D1313133

Please return/renew this item by the last
date shown. Books may also be renewed
by phone or Internet.

www.rbwm.gov.uk/web/onlinelibrary.htm

01628 796969 (library hours)

01628 633088 (24 hours)

38067100240488

ABOUT THE AUTHOR

Robert Wilson was born and bred in Ruislip, Middlesex. He is a regular walker, and has been a contributor to the 'Down Your Way' section of *Country Walking* magazine since 1990, covering Berkshire and neighbouring Buckinghamshire. He also wrote the companion volume *Walking in Buckinghamshire*, also published by Cicerone.

WALKING IN BERKSHIRE

by
Robert Wilson

2 POLICE SQUARE, MILNTHORPE, CUMBRIA LA7 7PY
www.cicerone.co.uk

© Robert Wilson 2003

ISBN 1 85284 335 7

A catalogue record for this book is available from the British Library

OS Ordnance Survey® This product includes mapping data licensed from Ordnance Survey® with the permission of the Controller of Her Majesty's Stationery Office. © Crown copyright 2002. *All rights reserved.*
Licence number PU100012932

Advice to Readers

Readers are advised that while every effort is taken by the author to ensure the accuracy of this guidebook, changes can occur which may affect the contents. It is advisable to check locally on transport, accommodation, shops, etc, but even rights of way can be altered. Paths can be affected by forestry work, landslip or changes of ownership.

The publisher would welcome notes of any such changes.

Front cover: The Thames Path near Henley

CONTENTS

Map showing location of walks

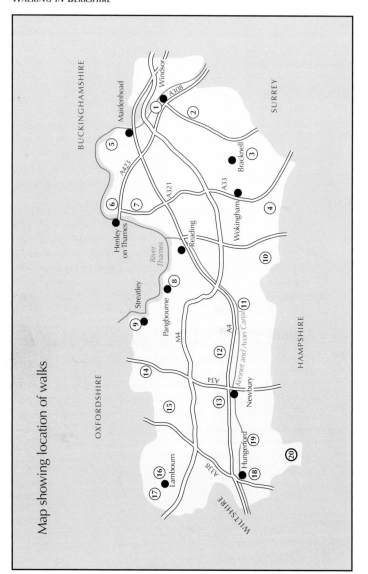

INTRODUCTION

With one end in the suburbs of London and the other in Wessex, Berkshire has a greater variety of scenery than its relatively small area would suggest (about 40 miles/65km from west to east and 12 miles/20km from north to south).

The walks in this guide cover the various scenic delights of Berkshire: the pinewoods and heathland in the south, to the peaceful, rural River Thames between Cookham and Streatley – ideal for chilling out on a hot summer's day; the majestic Downs – walking at its best with the sense of freedom gained from walking along wide tracks across open countryside; and the tranquil Kennet and Avon Canal – transformed from being the M4 of the eighteenth century to the haven for wildlife and leisure it is today. All this, together with some pretty villages, combine to make the Berkshire countryside special.

LANDSCAPE AND HISTORY

Geographically the county is split in two. South-east of the Reading–Slough axis the soil is clay-based, mixed with areas of sand and pebbles (mainly in the area around Bracknell and Crowthorne). Near the Thames between Henley and Maidenhead the terrain is chalk-based, an outcrop of the Chiltern Hills of Buckinghamshire and Oxfordshire on the other side of the river. West of Streatley are the superb chalk Wessex Downs, a continuation of the Chilterns, making for

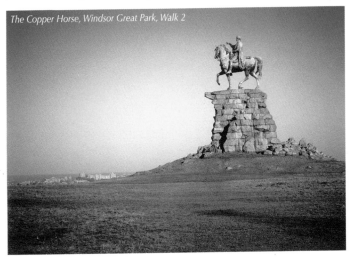

The Copper Horse, Windsor Great Park, Walk 2

Cockmarsh, Walk 5

wide open spaces. In the folds of the downs are some pretty villages. In contrast to the chalk downs is the recently restored Kennet and Avon Canal, the towpath offering a haven of peace and tranquility as it winds its way along the Kennet and Avon Valley.

Apart from the well-known Windsor and Eton there are few stately homes in Berkshire that are open to the public. The Duke of Wellington's Stratfield Saye (near Walk 10) is actually in Hampshire. Donnington Castle near Newbury (Walk 13) still bears the scars of the Civil War. The Craven Family were prominent in West Berkshire. Although Hamstead Lodge (Walk 19) has now been destroyed – only the

gateposts remain in splendid isolation in the middle of a field – the hunting lodge Ashdown House (Walk 17) is now owned by the National Trust. It is open on Wednesday and Saturday afternoons from April to October. The grand staircase surrounded by many portraits of the Craven family leads up to a balcony with superb views across the Downs. On a smaller scale, the Old Rectory at Farnborough (Walk 15) is visible from the road. It is not open to the public despite being owned by Sir John Betjeman in the period after the Second World War. The Thames Path crosses in front of Culham Court (also not open to the public).

There are a number of prehistoric monuments in Berkshire, notably the

Lambourn Downs, Walk 16

Iron Age forts at Caesar's Camp in Bracknell Forest (Walk 3) and Walbury Hill (Walk 20). Up on the Lambourn Downs is a series of Bronze Age burial mounds at Seven Barrows, to the north of Lambourn (Walk 17). Across the north of the county runs the Ridgeway, one of Europe's oldest roads (the earliest evidence of it being used was in the Bronze Age), a drovers' route across the chalk downs from Dorset to East Anglia (Walk 14).

USING THE GUIDE

The walks in this book are suitable for most weekend walkers, although a higher level of stamina is required for the slightly more challenging treks across the Downs. The walks range from 6 to 13 miles (9.5 to 21km) and all of them start and end at the same place (usually a car park).

The walks start in Windsor in the east and progress roughly westwards across the county, ending up at Inkpen near the Wiltshire border. The range of walks was chosen to cover a cross-section of the varied landscapes of the county. The factfiles at the start of each walk give the distance, approximate time for the average walker to complete the route (not allowing for stops), maps required, starting point with grid reference, and details of any refreshments – most of the walks have a pub or two along the way. Initial information in the sidebar

9

Donnington Castle, Walk 13

provides a brief overview of the route. The main route description begins with directions to your starting point. Points along the route where there is a significant change of direction are highlighted with emboldened letters (**A**, **B**) which correspond with those on the maps. Background information is given in indented type at relevant points in the route description.

MAPS

Berkshire is covered by the OS Landranger 1:50 000 sheets 174 and 175, which give a good general view of the area. However the Explorer sheets are better for walking as they also show the field boundaries. The county is cov-

ered by sheets 158, 159, 160, 170, 171 and 172. It is recommended that you take the Ordnance Survey map on the walk as well as this guidebook.

PATHS

Paths are generally well waymarked. Where the walk crosses farmland PLEASE keep to the path – remember that the farmer has to make a living out of the land you are walking across. Now that Berkshire has been divided into six unitary district councils (Bracknell, West Berkshire, Reading, Slough, Windsor and Maidenhead, and Wokingham) it is hoped that the standard of way-marking will be maintained.

Chaddleworth, Walk 15

Along the Kennet and Avon Canal, Walk 11

Coombe Gibbet, Walk 20

TRANSPORT

Thames Trains run a fairly reliable service across the county between Slough and Hungerford. Buses link the main towns with the smaller towns and villages. If you are intending to use public transport, it is advisable to make enquiries before you travel. The relevant sources of information are:

Thames Trains (National Enquiry Line):
   tel: 08457 48 49 50
   www.thamestrains.co.uk
Newbury Buses:
   tel: 01635 523700
Reading Buses:
   tel: 0118 959 4000
   www.reading-buses.co.uk

Car parking is not generally a problem. Please be considerate if parking on-road.

Bluebells near Frilsham, Walk 12

GENERAL

Most of the walks have pubs en route which all offer a range of bar food (though some might not be open on certain weekday lunchtimes) varying from filled rolls to gourmet meals. Otherwise there are still some village stores.

This is historically a Christian country and in each of the villages the church is the central building. However, not all the churches are always open. Most churches publish a small guidebook for a modest price, which goes towards maintaining the building.

1: Windsor and Eton

Distance:	6 miles/10km
Time:	2hr 30min
Map:	OS Landranger 175/Explorer 160
Start:	Car park by the recreation ground in Eton Wick (Grid Ref 948785)
Refreshments:	Various pubs and cafés in Windsor and Eton

Starting from Eton Wick, this level walk follows the Thames Path through the tourist honeypots of Windsor and Eton to the outskirts of Datchet, before returning across the playing fields of Eton. Some of the paths become waterlogged in the winter, so this walk is best saved for a hot summer's day (though you may not be able to move in Windsor and Eton for tourists!).

START: Car park by the recreation ground in Eton Wick. Eton Wick is reached from the A4 by heading south along the B3206 through Dorney, keeping to the main road through the village, then crossing Dorney Common. For public transport users, trains run from Waterloo and Paddington (branch line from Slough) to Windsor.

From the car park turn right along Haywards Mead, passing to the right of a modern church. Turn right along

Windsor Castle

a metalled track signposted to Windsor, Eton and Slough. Later pass alongside Boveney Ditch to reach the Thames Path on the Berkshire/Buckinghamshire border. (**A**) Turn left along the Thames Path. After passing underneath the A332 and railway the unmistakable landmark of Windsor Castle is seen ahead.

Windsor Castle has been a royal palace since the time of William I. In medieval times its site on a high chalk cliff above a bend in the Thames offered a strategic position. The earliest part of the castle was the Round Tower built for Edward III. The other main medieval building is St George's Chapel, started by Edward IV and completed by Henry VIII. Inside there are carved tombs and screens, the burial place of many English monarchs, together with the banners of the Knights of the Garter. Many of the English monarchs have made their mark on the castle, notably Charles II with the State Apartments.

Bear left past the Waterman's Arms to reach Eton High Street.

Eton is an attractive linear town dominated by Eton College at one end and Windsor Castle at the other. The High Street contains some fine old buildings, mostly dating from the

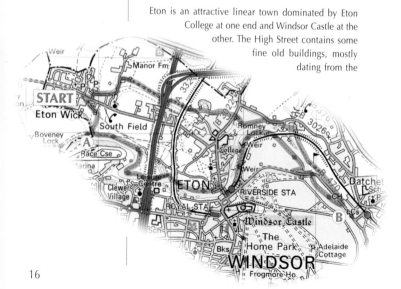

Windsor Bridge

eighteenth and nineteenth centuries. Windsor Bridge was built in 1822, although there has been a crossing at this point for over 800 years. The bridge was pedestrianised in 1970. To explore Windsor continue straight on over the bridge towards the castle and High Street. The town is perhaps best approached from this direction, passing some distinguished buildings. The High Street contains some individual shops, with an attractive modern precinct around the central station. Set into the pavement in the High Street is a clock.

To continue the walk turn left along Thames Side on the Windsor Bank. Bear left along the Thames Path between the river and Riverside Station. Ignore a footbridge at Romney Lock. Turn right through a kissing gate (signposted 'Thames Path to Datchet'). Pass under the railway and continue along the edge of Home Park, with Windsor Castle as a backdrop. Further on, Victoria Bridge (the B470) is reached. Bear right across the grass

The Thames near Windsor

and up the embankment to the white railings. Turn left across the bridge, then right down some steps on the other side. This path leads to the outskirts of Datchet.

> Datchet is a Victorian riverside town, centred around an older village green. The town has some literary associations – it was mentioned in Jerome K Jerome's *Three Men in a Boat*. What is now the B470 was 'Datchet Lane' in Shakespeare's *Merry Wives of Windsor*.

The walk leaves the Thames Path at this point. (**B**) Cross over the B470 and turn left by the footpath sign opposite. After passing through a spinney, the walk follows the left-hand edge of a golf course. Further on, bear right along a track. Pass underneath the railway. Turn left over a footbridge, crossing a channel which has been dug to alleviate flood problems in the area. Continue along the left-hand edge of the field. Cross over a track to reach Eton College Boathouse and the main road. Turn left along a public footpath sign to cross the playing fields of Eton.

The playing fields of Eton

19

According to Wellington, the battle of Waterloo was won on the playing fields of Eton. The playing fields, together with the watermeadows to the west of the town, are dominated by Eton College Chapel. Eton College was founded by Henry VI in 1440 and is the most famous public school in the world.

At a bridge turn sharp right, then left. On your left, just before the road, is the Old Cricket Pavilion. Cross over the road to a gate by a public footpath sign. Cross the field to a further public footpath sign. Bear left along a permissive path (stream on left, ignore a footbridge) to reach some houses. Turn right at a T-junction. After passing underneath the railway continue straight on along a track between fields. Further on, turn left to pass underneath the A332, then continue alongside a fence on your left. Go straight on over a cross-paths to reach a lane. Turn left along this lane to reach the outskirts of Eton Wick. As the lane bends right to skirt the built-up area, there is still a rural outlook to the right. The lane bends left by the Old Wheel Bush. Turn right along the main road and soon the modern church at the start is reached.

2: Windsor Great Park

Distance:	6.5 miles/11km
Time:	2hr 40min
Map:	OS Landranger 175/Explorer 160
Start:	Savill Gardens Car Park (Grid Ref 977705)
Refreshments:	Savill Gardens Restaurant and shop

START: Savill Gardens Car Park. From Windsor take the A308 towards Staines. Savill Gardens are signposted from the town. The fee-paying car park is open until dusk – the exact closing time is shown at the entrance. For public transport users the nearest train station is in Windsor. On leaving the car park bear right to the obelisk, then continue down a track to a bridge.

Unlike Home Park, much of Windsor Great Park is open to the public. The park owes its beauty to generations of foresters and landscape gardeners. Some of the walk is along metalled drives which makes this suitable for a winter walk. The route includes the Copper Horse statue with its superb vista along the Long Walk towards Windsor Castle. The return is through the famous Valley Gardens.

The obelisk commemorates the Duke of Cumberland, who was made Park Ranger after his military success at the battle of Culloden in 1746. The layout of the park is largely due to the duke. He appointed the architect and artist Thomas Stanby as Deputy Ranger. Between them they designed winding vistas, planted conifers and created Virginia Water.

After crossing the bridge proceed along the right-hand edge of Smith's Lawn. Over to the left is the polo pitch. At a T-junction turn right through Cumberland Gate. Further on, the track bends right to skirt around the Royal Lodge. At the next cross-tracks, two pink-washed neo-Georgian lodges are passed – these were built by Tatchell. From the cross-tracks bear left to a deer gate, then follow the metalled drive through the park. The track later bears round to the left with a panoramic view of Windsor.

The Obelisk, Windsor Great Park

Windsor Great Park is haunted by Herne the Hunter. He is seen as a deer who appears to glow near the site of a great oak tree. He wears a large chain with antlers growing out of his head. It is thought that Herne was a royal hunter who saved the king's life by placing his body between a wounded stag and the monarch. A wizard told the king that the only way to save Herne was to cut off the stag's antlers and tie them to the hunter's head.

Although Herne is associated with Richard II, he was in the park centuries earlier. The stag's antlers associate him with Cernunnos, the Celtic god of the underworld. He once worshipped in the park and his ghost guards an ancient shrine.

(**A**) Soon the Long Walk is reached. Here turn left uphill to the Copper Horse, and on to the Three Castles Path (although waymarking is nonexistent). From the statue there is a superb vista along the Long Walk into Windsor.

Charles II planted the Long Walk in 1685 with gigantic elm trees. This was part of the first attempt to turn the ancient terrace into a park. The elms were felled in 1945

The Long Walk

and replaced with plane and chestnut trees. The statue was finished in 1831 and is now known as the Copper Horse. It stands on a pedestal of rough stones and is visible throughout the park. From as far away as Windsor Castle it is recognisable as a horse and rider.

From the statue continue straight on down the hill to a deer gate, then along a wide track between fences. This can be quite boggy after a wet spell. After passing Ox Pond on the right the route returns to firmer terrain as it rises to a drive.

Ahead is Cumberland Lodge, built during the reign of Charles II. The Duke of Cumberland lived here when he was the Park Ranger. Very little of the original building remains as it was damaged by fire in 1811. It was enlarged in 1870 and later remodelled after having been restored after the fire.

Turn right along a drive, passing to the right of Chaplin's Lodge. Where the drive bends right, fork left along a track. Turn left at a cross-paths, along Duke's Lane.

Alongside Duke's Lane is a marker stating that some of

the oak trees were planted in 1751. Together with the deer, the oak trees have been part of the park since ancient times. The trees provided firewood, fencing and fodder for the local people who grazed their animals in the park. The fencing was made from the new branches, which grew after 'pollarding' – when the lower boughs were removed out of the way of grazing animals.

(**B**) After crossing a stream turn left along a track through the woods. This is also used by riders, so keep alongside the edge. In a dip turn left along a grassy ride, passing a 'No Entry for Horses' sign. Soon the western edge of Virginia Water appears on the right. At the end of the ride turn left along a drive. Further on, this drive bends right to a bridge. After crossing this bridge turn right, then left into Valley Gardens. Where the path forks take the right fork, keeping to the main path, heedless of all turnings off.

The Valley Gardens were created by Sir Eric Savill. Work started in 1947 clearing the woodland and thick undergrowth. The gardens contain rhododendron bushes and

The Valley Gardens

25

some fine magnolias. As you walk through the gardens, which are less formal than the Savill Gardens, there are occasional glimpses of Virginia Water.

The Totem Pole, the Valley Gardens

At the top of the rise turn right along a drive signposted to the Totem Pole. Where the drive forks, take the left fork.

The Totem Pole was presented to the Queen in 1958 on the centenary of British Columbia. It is 100ft/30m high and made from western red cedar. It is decorated with Pacific Coast Indian art.

(**C**) At the Totem Pole turn left along a track signposted to Savill Gardens and car park. At the top of the rise, at a cross-tracks, continue straight on past a sign proclaiming 'No Entry for Garden Visitors' Cars'. Soon the Obelisk Pond is reached and the obelisk looms ahead. Bear right, back to the car park.

3: The Look Out, Swinley Forest

Distance:	6¼ miles/10km
Time:	2hr 30min
Map:	OS Landranger 175/Explorer 160
Start:	Car park at the Look Out Discovery Centre (Grid Ref 877662)
Refreshments:	Café at the Look Out Discovery Centre

The Look Out is a heritage centre located in Swinley Forest, near Bracknell. There is an extensive network of tracks through the forest, which is popular with walkers (with or without dogs), riders and mountain bikers. The walk includes the Iron Age fort at Caesar's Camp and part of the Devil's Highway, a former Roman road.

START: Car park at the Look Out Discovery Centre. The Look Out is reached from Windsor by proceeding south-west across Windsor Great Park on the A322 or the B3022 (past Legoland) towards Ascot, then turning right onto the A329 towards Bracknell. On the outskirts of Bracknell turn left onto the B3430 (the Look Out is signposted from here). The Look Out is on the left after crossing the A322.

From the car park turn right towards the heritage centre, then pass between the centre and the picnic area. Dogs are not allowed in the picnic area but dog walkers can start by heading south-east along the nature trail, then turning right at the first cross-paths. Turn right at the next cross-paths to return to the heritage centre.

The heritage centre is aimed at families and includes a tourist information centre, a shop and a café. It is open from 10am to 6pm. A large-scale map showing all the forest tracks is available here. Although the heritage centre is popular with families at weekends, walk a few hundred yards into the forest and the hordes of kids disappear!

On leaving the picnic area bear right over a track along the Ramblers Route (linking the Look Out to the Devil's Highway). Continue along the Heritage Trail. Where the track forks, keep going straight on. At the next cross-paths turn right, soon passing a pond. Turn right at a cross-tracks near the top of the rise. Where the track bends right continue straight on downhill on a smaller path along the eastern edge of Caesar's Camp.

> Caesar's Camp is a small Iron Age hill fort, about 20 acres in size. There are two large entrances on the western and eastern edges, together with a prominent counterscarp bank. It has been restored in recent years. Alongside the path is an information board explaining the history of the fort including an impression of how the fort appeared in the Iron Age.

Turn left through a kissing gate to enter Caesar's Camp. At the top turn right at a T-junction to reach the northern edge of the fort. (**A**) At the bottom cross over a stile and turn left along the second track close to the western edge

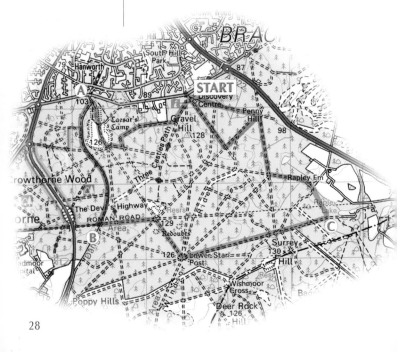

of Caesar's Camp. Continue straight on over two cross-tracks. After passing a clearing, Wickham Bushes, the track descends to the Devil's Highway.

Caesar's Camp

> The Devil's Highway is a Roman road built between London and Silchester. The road was so named by the locals after the Romans left – they thought that only the devil could have built it!

(**B**) Turn left along the Devil's Highway, climbing steeply at first to reach the Upper Star Post. Turn right along the track signposted to the Lower Star Post. At the Lower Star Post, another multi-track junction, take the third turn on the left (the Lake Ride) – it's the one immediately to the left of the track with the telegraph lines. Continue

29

straight on over a major cross-paths (even though the left-hand track is signposted as leading back to the Look Out).

> The track to the left is part of the Mountain Bike Trail and connects the Look Out with the designated mountain bike area to the south of the Lake Ride. Mountain bikes are available for hire at the heritage centre.

(**C**) Where the track bends right turn left along a smaller path into the trees by a 'No Horses' notice. Further on, the path bends left along the edge of the forest. To the right is a view across open farmland to Rapley's Farm – a change of scene from the forest. Later the track bears left back into the middle of the forest. Ignore a track going off to the right, although a short detour will bring you to

Wickham Bushes

the Mill Pond. Turn right at a major cross-tracks (sign-posted back to the Look Out) – Bracknell Road. You realise that you are nearly back to the start when you pass some posts marking the Junior Nature Trail! At the next cross-tracks, Penny Hill, turn left, then right back to the heritage centre and car park.

4: Finchampstead Ridges

Set in the heathlands near the Hampshire border, this is an ideal winter's walk as the sandy soil drains away the rain more effectively than the clays around Windsor. Starting around Finchampstead Ridges, the route explores the older part of Finchampstead before descending to the Blackwater Lakes, a nature reserve around some disused gravel pits which have been turned into lakes.

Distance:	6 miles/9.5km
Time:	2hr 30min
Map:	OS Landranger 175/Explorer 160
Start:	National Trust car park at Finchampstead Ridges (Grid Ref 813635)
Refreshments:	The Queen's Oak, Finchampstead

START: The National Trust car park at Finchampstead Ridges. From Wokingham proceed south on the A321 towards Crowthorne, turning right along the B3348 (Wellingtonia Avenue) – it's the roundabout after the double roundabout. From Reading take the A327 towards Arborfield Cross. Turn left to Finchampstead (the B3348). In the village turn left, then right. There is a train station in Wokingham, and buses 142 and 144 from the town stop in Finchampstead.

From the National Trust car park head north along a path through the woods, starting from the middle entrance. Turn left at a broad cross-tracks, then right at the next cross-tracks past a National Trust notice. Soon pass a lake in its tranquil setting on the left. Continue straight on over the first cross-tracks (part of the Devil's Highway). At the next cross-tracks turn left along a metalled track. (**A**) Further on, turn left along Wick Lane. Where the lane bends left turn right along a narrower path, soon climbing gently through the woods. At the top of the rise bear left in the direction of a public footpath sign past Warren Crest Farm. Pass through a kissing gate and continue along the left-hand edge of the field to reach the road. Ahead is the tower of Finchampstead church. Cross the road to the kissing gate opposite, then cross the field diagonally (in the direction of a public footpath sign) to the opposite corner. Turn right along the lane, climbing up to Finchampstead church and the Queen's Oak pub.

Finchampstead church is built on the site of an ancient earthwork with fine views across surrounding countryside. The main body of the church is of Norman origin, with a Perpendicular north window and chancel arch. The north door is also of the Perpendicular style but dated 1590. The brick tower (laid in English bend) was added in 1720. Near the church is the Queen's Oak pub, offering a range of bar food.

The Heath Pond,
Finchampstead Ridges

At the Queen's Oak continue straight on up the lane to the church. Turn left through the churchyard. The path leads down some steps to a kissing gate. Ahead is a fine view across to the Blackwater Valley and Hampshire beyond. Ignore a footpath going off to the right. At the bottom turn right along a road (the B3348) then left along Longwater Lane. Continue straight on over the second main road (the B3016) along Cricket Hill.

(**B**) Public transport users can start the walk at this point. Follow the lane, Cricket Hill, round to the left. Turn right along a gravel path just after Honeysuckle Cottage past a small car park. Turn left at a T-junction at the end of the second lake. Where the path forks at a footbridge, take the left fork (do not cross over the bridge).

This section of the walk passes through the Blackwater Lakes Nature Reserve. The lakes are man-made using disused quarry pits. The lakes are popular with bird watchers and there are several hides along the lakesides, although these are not open to the public. Angling is prohibited alongside the lakes but the Blackwater River, which flows between the lakes, often has anglers along its banks.

(**C**) Turn sharp left by a circular walk noticeboard just before the road (the B3272). Pass alongside the eastern edge of the lakes. At a lane continue straight on along the left-hand side of the field opposite. Turn left along the second lane. Where the lane bends left bear right

Finchampstead church

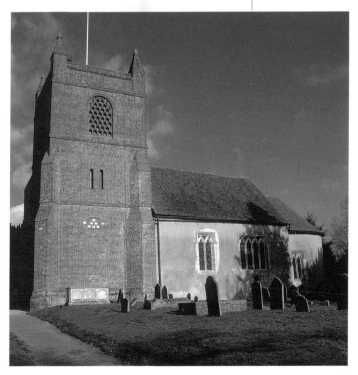

Across the Blackwater Lakes

along a track by a public footpath sign. Further on, the path bends right and starts to climb.

> At the top is a superb view left, across to the Blackwater Lakes in the valley below.

At a T-junction turn right along a track. Ignore a footpath going off to the left.
  Soon the B3348 is reached.

> This road is also known as Wellingtonia Avenue and is flanked by a series of Sequoia pines, a smaller version of the large evergreen trees native to California. The tree was introduced to Britain in 1853, both the road and the line of trees are named after the Duke of Wellington. On

a lighter note, this was the road that Pinky and Perky drove along in the 1960s children's TV series.

Cross over this road and continue along the track opposite. There is a large mound of earth at the start of the track to prevent certain vehicles from using it (it is classified as a 'road used as a public path' on the Ordnance Survey map). Bear left through the trees back to the start. The car park is visible from the track.

5: Cookham

Cookham is an attractive Thames-side village, which is popular with tourists especially in the summer months. The village was made famous by the painter Sir Stanley Spencer who lived in the village and set many of his paintings there. The old Methodist chapel where he worshipped has been turned into a museum of some of his works and artefacts. It is well worth a visit, either before or after the walk. The walk itself leads up to Cookham Rise before crossing the fields to Cookham Dean, much of which is owned by the National Trust. A superb balcony path along the edge of the escarpment through Quarry Wood (with fine views across to the Chilterns) leads you to Winter Hill. The return to Cookham is along the Thames.

Distance:	7 miles/10.5km
Time:	3hr
Map:	OS Landranger 175/Explorer 172
Start:	National Trust car park on Cookham Moor (Grid Ref 893853)
Refreshments:	The Jolly Farmer, Cookham Dean; The Bounty by the Thames; various pubs and cafés in Cookham

START: The National Trust car park on Cookham Moor to the west of the village at the end of the High Street. Cookham is on the main A4094 road between Maidenhead and Bourne End. Cookham Station is on the branch line from Maidenhead to Marlow.

From the National Trust car park cross over the road to the old bridge. Turn right along the track then on along the road to Cookham Rise. After crossing the railway turn left along High Road. Ignore all turnings off.

By Cookham Rise school is the cottage where Stanley Spencer worked and died. When he was a student at the Slade he used to commute from Cookham every day.

At the end, turn right then left along a track by a public footpath sign. This leads to the Church of St John the Baptist, Cookham Dean, and the Jolly Farmer pub. The pub was 'bought for the village by the village' when Courage sold the pub in 1987. Turn right along the road, then left along a track past the war memorial. Turn left by a public footpath sign to the Inn on the Green restaurant, then continue along a path through a spinney. Bear right to a squeeze stile. Cross the field to a cross-paths in a dip and on up the other side to reach a road. Turn left along this road for a few yards, then turn right along the track into Bisham Woods (also known as Quarry Wood). Ignore the first path going off to the right.

Quarry Wood is one of the most impressive landscape features in Berkshire, forming the backdrop to Bisham church and abbey. The woods were once part of the abbey estate and are now a designated a Site of Special Scientific Interest. They are managed to meet both forestry and conservation objectives. Kenneth Graham, who was brought up in Cookham Dean, walked in these woods as a child, and they were the inspiration for the 'Wild Wood' in *The Wind in the Willows*.

(**A**) At a five-point junction turn right. Ignore paths going off to the right. The track swings left to a crest. Follow the track round to the right (past a yellow waymark post) along the top of the escarpment. There are spectacular views across to the Chilterns. Fork left by a white arrow on a tree. Turn right along the road for a few paces, then bear left by a public footpath sign along the path parallel to the road (in the same direction as before along the top edge of the escarpment). Further on, the path swings right to a gravel drive. Follow the drive out to the road then left along the road to the viewpoint on Winter Hill.

> From here there are superb wide-reaching views across and along the Thames Valley.

After passing Stonehouse Lane bear left down a track (by a public footpath sign) to reach the National Trust owned Cockmarsh. Keep to the main track downhill. At the bottom the path bends left to a kissing gate and on across the field to a Thames-side cottage.

The Thames near Cookham

> The kissing gate was erected in memory of Henry Bridges Fearon (1907–95) who as the writer 'Fieldfare'

brought his love of the English countryside to thousands of walkers.

At the public footpath sign the path bends right to join the Thames towpath. Soon the Bounty pub is reached.

The Bounty is not accessible by road. Inside it is covered with various boating memorabilia. The pub caters for the boating crowd as well as walkers along the Thames Path. It serves a variety of food and is recommended for a break before the final stretch back to Cookham. A little further on is the Bourne End railway bridge, a single-track structure forming part of the Maidenhead–Bourne End–Marlow shuttle. The Thames Path now runs alongside the track. Over to the right, on the chalk slopes of Cockmarsh, is a group of round barrows, the largest of which is 90ft/27m across. When three of the barrows were excavated in the nineteenth century, two of them were found to be Bronze Age burial mounds.

Follow the Thames Path back towards Cookham. Further on, the path swings round to the left with Cookham church and bridge coming into view. Near the bridge turn right to enter the churchyard (still on the Thames Path).

The bridge is of original design (wood and cast iron) and was built in 1867. There was a toll until the 1940s. Holy Trinity Church, Cookham, dates from the thirteenth century (Early English). Inside is a copy of Stanley Spencer's The Last Supper. The original is in the Stanley Spencer museum (when it is not out on loan). A lot of Spencer's paintings are of Biblical scenes, often in a Cookham setting as he often saw Cookham as a scene of heavenly visitation. The Stanley Spencer Gallery, at the end of the High Street (at the junction with the main road), includes a selection of his drawings and paintings, together with some of his memorabilia including the pram in which he transported his equipment. The largest canvas on show is the unfinished Christ Preaching at Cookham Regatta.

The village itself has not lost its character, even

Cookham church

though the High Street houses have been turned into shops (all highly individual of course!).

On leaving the churchyard bear left past the timber-framed Church Gate House to reach the A4094. Turn right along this road, then right along the High Street to return to Cookham Moor and the car park. For the station, continue straight on along the road to Cookham Rise.

6: Remenham Hill

Distance:	6¼ miles/10km
Time:	2hr 30min
Map:	OS Landranger 175 Explorer 171
Start:	The walkers' car park near Mill End (Grid Ref 785854)
Refreshments:	The Flower Pot, Aston; various pubs and cafés in Henley

Remenham consists of three hamlets in a wide loop of the Thames east of Henley. Starting from Mill End, on the Buckinghamshire side of the river, the walk crosses into Berkshire at Hambleden Lock before passing in front of the impressive Culham Court. The climb up to Remenham Hill is rewarded with superb views across to the most attractive part of the Chilterns. The return is along by the river.

START: The free walkers' car park near Mill End at the southern end of the Hambleden Valley. Mill End is reached by proceeding north from Henley along the A4155 towards Marlow. After about 3 miles/5km turn left along the Hambleden Valley road. The car park is 600yds/m on the left. There are train stations at both Henley and Marlow, with a bus service linking both towns. There is a bus stop at Mill End.

From the Mill End car park turn right along the Hambleden Valley road south towards Mill End. Turn right along the A4155 for a few paces, then left by a public footpath sign, passing Hambleden Mill to cross the river to Hambleden Lock.

> The weatherboarded mill (built in 1338) was powered by a water turbine and was worked until 1955. It has now been converted into luxury apartments and is one of the most photogenic spots in the Chilterns. The river is crossed via a metal walkway which passes close to the weir.

Turn left along the Thames Path. Follow the track round to the right when the Thames Path continues straight on to reach the hamlet of Aston. Turn left down the lane past the Flower Pot inn.

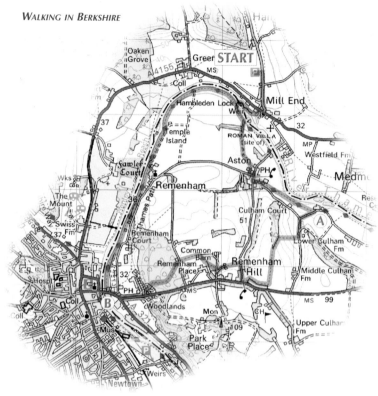

The Flower Pot is owned by Henley Brewery and is popular with fishing and boating parties. Inside it is wonderfully old-fashioned and serves a selection of ales and bar food.

At the pub turn right along Aston Lane, then left along a track by a Thames Path sign. Where the track bends right continue straight on along a path. The path bears left through a kissing gate to pass in front of Culham Court.

To the left is a fine view up the Hambleden Valley. Culham Court is an impressive red-brick building set well above the river. It was built in 1770–71 though the architect is not known. It is not open to the public.

Culham Court

Continue across the fields in the same direction as before. (**A**) Turn sharp right at a T-junction (fence on your right), then left along a track at the next T-junction. After a short climb turn right by a public footpath sign into a dip and on up the other side along the right-hand edge of the field. Turn left along the outside edge of the wood, still climbing.

> At the top there is a superb view across the southern Chilterns from Fawley to Medmenham, whilst in the other direction the twin wooded peaks of Ashley Hill and Bowsey Hill are seen.

Pass through a hedge gap and continue along a track (hedge now on left). Just before the road turn right along a path along the back of some gardens. At a stile turn left towards the road, then the path bends right to a stile. Turn right along Aston Lane. At the end of the houses turn left along a path between fences. Turn right along a path between a hedge and a fence at the top of the rise. The path bears left through the wood, then on between another fence and hedge. At a gate turn left across the field to a stile and onto a lane. Turn left along the lane for

Temple Island

a few paces then bear right over a stile (by a public foot-path sign) into the woods. Continue straight on over a cross-tracks in the middle of the wood, then fork left by a white arrow on a tree soon descending towards Henley. From the woods there is a fine view of Henley over to the right. On leaving the wood continue straight on over a drive to reach the A4130. Turn right, downhill, towards Henley. (**B**) Just before the bridge turn right along the Thames Path. The path bears left to reach the riverside.

> This part of the river is part of the Henley Regatta course, the races being held between Henley Bridge and Temple Island. The regatta takes place in the first week of July each year and for a few weeks either side the grass areas are covered with stands and hospitality marquees. During these weeks the riverside path is usually closed although if this is the case the path is likely to be diverted (especially as it's a National Trail). The first Oxford versus Cambridge Boat Race was run along this stretch of the river (between Henley and Hambleden Lock) in 1829 before it was transferred to the stretch between Putney and Mortlake.

Follow the riverside path for 2½ miles/4km back to Hambleden Lock.

> The Church of St Nicholas, Remenham, is passed. The present building was rebuilt in 1870. A large two-light window on the northern side remains, along with a Norman apse. Ahead is Temple Island, built in 1771 by James Wyatt. The folly originally belonged to Fawley Court, on the Buckinghamshire side of the river. It is a fishing lodge with a cupola containing a statue of a naked lady. Temple Island is at the end of the mile-long straight that is the Henley Regatta course.

After Temple Island the bitumen ends and the path and river swing right towards Hambleden Lock. A gate brings you to the lockside. Turn left along the metal walkway which leads across the river, passing close to the white

water of Hambleden Weir towards Hambleden Mill and out to the A4155. Turn right for a few paces, then left along the Hambleden Valley road back to the start.

Hembleden Mill

7: Wargrave and Bowsey Hill

Wargrave is a riverside village, Edwardian in appearance. The Thames has moulded the character of the village which is popular in summer with the boating crowd and day-trippers. The walk soon leaves the village behind, with the first of many views across the Thames Valley before heading across the fields to the twin wooded peaks of Bowsey Hill and Ashley Hill. About halfway round is one of the remotest pubs in Berkshire, the Dewdrop Inn, built as an alehouse for forestry workers. Just before the return to Wargrave is the pretty village of Crazies Hill with Rebecca's Well.

Distance:	8 miles/13km
Time:	3hr
Map:	OS Landranger 175/Explorer 159, 171 and 172
Start:	Car park in Wargrave (Grid Ref 786785)
Refreshments:	The Dewdrop Inn, Ashley Hill; various pubs in Wargrave

START: The car park in Wargrave. Wargrave is reached from Henley by taking the A321 south (which crosses the main A4 at Twyford). For the car park turn left at the traffic lights in the village centre (if coming from Henley). The pay-and-display car park is on the left almost immediately. There are also a couple of lay-bys on the north side of the village, east of Wargrave Manor, one at the start of the path leading to Bowsey Hill. Wargrave Station is on the Reading to Henley branch line and is situated to the west of the village (Grid Ref 781783).

Turn left out of the car park, ignoring the initial turnings off. Where the road bends right turn left up Dark Lane. At the top of the rise is a fine view to the left across the Thames Valley. Turn right at a T-junction past the drive to Wargrave Manor (seen on the return). Where the road bends right, just after Purfield Drive, turn left at a public footpath sign. Here is a small lay-by where a few cars can be left. Cross the field to a kissing gate, then continue along the right-hand edge of the next field towards Bowsey Hill ahead. This path is popular with local dog walkers. Ignore a footpath going off to the left. A little further on turn right over a stile and continue along the outside edge of the wood. At a cross-paths turn right along a track, then left by a public footpath sign, along the right-hand edge of the field.

Enter the woods by a kissing gate and continue along the inside edge of the wood (NOT the path that bears off to the left towards the middle of the woods). Soon leave the wood and continue along a track between fences. The path then re-enters the woods and starts to climb Bowsey Hill. At the top of the rise turn right at a T-junction, then left along a track past some old barns. Ignore a path going off to the left. At a cross-tracks turn right for a few paces then turn left along track 4. At the wood edge turn left at a T-junction, then turn right over a stile. Cross the field to the white house ahead. Pass over two stiles and continue along the track ahead, passing to the right of the white cottage, then past some more pretty cottages. When the main road is reached turn left for a few paces, then right over a stile.

(**A**) In the middle of the field turn left (there is a white arrow on a telegraph pole to guide you) heading for a gate in the corner of the field by some old farming machinery. Follow the drive for a few paces, then turn left over a stile along by a fence on your right – the Recreational Route. Further on, the hedge is on your left as you start to

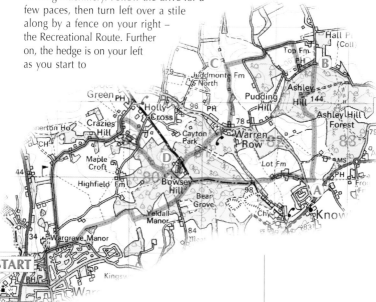

climb Ashley Hill. Cross over a stile into the woods. Continue straight on over a cross-paths near the top, to reach a large house at the summit of Ashley Hill.

> This house is called Keeper's Cottage, although it has been recently enlarged and is rather more grandiose these days. The porch is in neo-classical style.

Turn right at a T-junction after passing the house, which leads to the drive outside the main gates. After about 200yds/m turn left by a public footpath sign. (**B**) At the bottom turn left along a metalled track. Turn right by a public bridleway sign past the Dewdrop Inn.

Looking across to Bowsey Hill

> The Dewdrop Inn is one of the remotest pubs in Berkshire. It was built as an alehouse for forestry workers in about 1700. Inside it is small but offers a wide range

A tranquil corner of Bowsey Hill

of bar food and is ideal for a break at about the halfway stage. A great pub (even if it does share its name with the bar in the 1970s American soap *The Waltons*!).

At the end of the track turn left. Further on, turn left along a concrete track. When the track bends left continue straight on downhill on a wide path between fences. To the right is a view across to the Chilterns. (**C**) At the bottom turn left along a track for a few paces then bear right to a path between fences which runs parallel to the track (and is nowhere near as muddy!). By a stile on the left the path bears right and leads to Warren Row.

Warren Row is a hamlet set between Bowsey Hill and Ashley Hill. It contains several cottages, a corrugated-iron church and an up-market pub.

Turn right along the road in Warren Row, then left at a

public footpath sign. Follow the marked track into the woods, past a pit on the left, eventually climbing up to the summit of Bowsey Hill. At the top turn right, then sharp left. (**D**) At the end of the track turn right along a (rather muddy) path along the backs of the gardens. This path later swings left. At a T-junction turn right, then continue straight on over a cross-paths after a few paces. Follow the waymarked path through the woods to a peaceful lane. Turn right along this lane, then left along a track after about 20yds/m. Soon Rebecca's Well is reached.

> Rebecca's Well consists of a spring with a small cover built over it to protect the water from autumn leaves and debris from the trees above. The gabled cover was built in about 1870 and was later painted with the scene from the Book of Genesis (chapter 24) where Isaac, a servant of Abraham, is praying by a spring and a local girl, Rebecca, fills up her jar with water from the spring and gives Isaac (and his camels) a drink of water from her jar – hence the name. Once the spring was the only source of water for the people of Crazies Hill.

Ignore a footpath going off to the left to reach the houses of Crazies Hill.

> Crazies Hill is named after the buttercups which used to grow around the village. It was believed that wearing a buttercup chain round the neck was a cure for lunacy.

Turn left along the quiet lane out of the village. To the left is Gibstroude Farm, a riding centre which contains an all-weather horse track. The lane later bends left, back towards Wargrave.

> To the right is a view across to Harpsden, on the outskirts of the Chilterns, while on the left is Bowsey Hill. Further on, Wargrave Manor is seen. It was built in the early nineteenth century and included a long veranda and two bay wings. The house is privately owned.

At a T-junction turn right, rejoining the outward route. By the gates to Wargrave Manor turn left along Dark Lane. Retrace your steps back to the car park.

Rebecca's Well, Crazies Hill

Wargrave church is on the road between the station and the main village street. It was rebuilt after the original church was burnt down in 1914, with only the Norman tower remaining from the original building. It is claimed that the arsonists were a bunch of militant suffragettes who wanted to avenge the vicar for refusing to remove the word 'obey' from the marriage service. The church-yard contains the grave of the Earl of Barrymore, who was something of a maverick. He lived in the village towards the end of the eighteenth century and built a theatre nearby which was a great success on its opening night in 1791. However, the earl died in 1793 and it was discovered that he had spent £250,000 on the theatre and his sporting pursuits. He was buried before his creditors could kidnap his body and hold it to ransom until his debts were paid, taking the phrase 'pound of flesh' literally!

8: Pangbourne

Distance:	7½ miles/12km
Time:	3hr
Map:	OS Landranger 175/Explorer 159
Start:	Car park by Whitchurch Bridge (Grid Ref 635767)
Refreshments:	The Greyhound, Tidmarsh; various pubs and cafés in Pangbourne

START: The pay-and-display car park by Whitchurch Bridge. Further car parking is available by the village hall (Grid Ref 635765). Pangbourne is reached from Reading by proceeding west along the A4 (Junction 12 of the M4) then heading north along the A340. For the car park turn right along the A349, then left by W H Smith. The car park is just before Whitchurch Bridge. Whitchurch Bridge is one of the last remaining toll bridges across the Thames – the toll is a nominal 10p either way. Pangbourne Station is along the road from the village hall.

From the car park head north turning left out of the car park to reach the high street. Cross over the road (there is a zebra crossing a few yards away) and continue along The Moors (past W H Smith). This quiet track passes some pretty cottages. Continue along the footpath at the end of the cottages. Pass through a kissing gate and cross the field to the River Pang. Continue alongside the riverbank (river on right). Soon a footbridge is reached. Turn right over this bridge, a truly tranquil spot so close to the town and main road. After crossing the bridge turn left (river now on left). Where the river bends left continue straight on across the field to a stile, then on to a further stile. Turn left at a T-junction. At the end of the track turn right along a path between a fence and hedge, which leads out to the main

Pangbourne is a large village alongside the river. Kenneth Graham, author of *The Wind in the Willows*, lived here. Although the village itself is busier these days, there is still an air of Edwardian gentility along by the river. The riverside is a popular place for relaxation on a summer's afternoon, a scene which would have inspired an impressionist painter. The walk starts along the tranquil Pang Valley before climbing to the outskirts of Reading (thankfully briefly!) before heading back towards the river, with fine views across to the Chilterns and Wessex Downs. The return to Pangbourne is alongside the river.

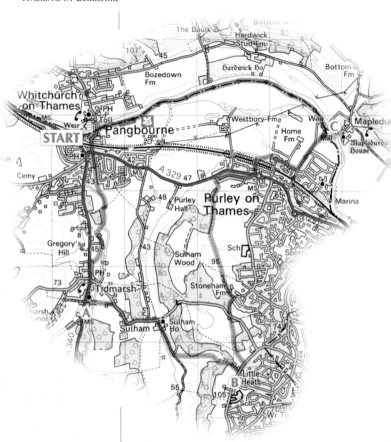

road in the village of Tidmarsh. Turn left along the road through the village.

The cottages alongside the main road were once the estate cottages for Tidmarsh Manor. The village also contains the only pub on the walk, the Greyhound, which offers a good selection of bar food – the only drawback is that it's only just over a mile into the walk! However, there is only one climb on the remainder of the walk, which isn't too challenging (unless you over-indulge here!).

(**A**) Turn left down the lane next to the pub (signposted to Sulham and Tilehurst). Turn left by a public footpath sign, crossing the River Pang by a footbridge. Continue alongside the right-hand edge of the field, passing a couple of pill-boxes. Cross over a stream, the path passing alongside the left-hand edge of the next field. At a lane turn left, then right over a stile. When the path bends left continue straight on along a path between fences. At the end of the path cross over a lane and continue along the track opposite, past Sulham church.

Sulham church was built in the nineteenth century and is set in a sloping churchyard. Unusually these days, it is kept open. Inside there is a triple rood screen (three pointed arches almost stretching from the floor to the roof) at the entrance to the chancel. The chancel itself is painted blue with gold stars.

The peaceful River Pang

*The chancel,
Sulham church*

Turn left by a public footpath sign just before the track bends left. Follow the grassy track to the top of the rise, then bear left alongside the outside edge of the wood. The tower-like structure over to the right is a dovecote. Further on, bear right across the field in the direction of a public footpath sign. The path is not clear but the route is towards the left-hand edge of the wood in the dip, then across the field to a stile in the opposite corner. Follow the path up through the wood, climbing steadily. Ignore a permissive path going off to the left. At the top continue along a drive, leading out to a road. Turn left along this road, which actually runs along the edge of Reading.

(**B**) Turn left over a stile along the right-hand edge of the field. Ignore the path going off to the left. Where the hedge bends right continue straight on across the field to a stile (to the right of the house ahead). The path leads through the spinney out to a lane. Bear left along Long Lane opposite. Turn left along a track by a public footpath sign in the dip. Carry straight on over a cross-tracks at the top of a gentle rise. Ahead is a fine view across to the Chilterns. The path later follows the outside edge of Mosshall Wood. Ignore a path going off into the wood. At the end of the wood the path bends left, still hugging the outside edge of the wood. Turn right across the field to a strip of woodland by a large pit on your left. The pit is popular with local mountain bikers.

Follow the path through this strip of woodland, then down along the right-hand edge of the field. To the left is a view up the Thames Valley towards the Wessex Downs. Turn right through a squeeze stile to a residential road, parallel to the A329. Continue along this road. Further on, it bends left to reach the A329. Turn right along this main road for a few yards, then turn left by a public bridleway sign (just before a roundabout – there is a traffic island in the middle of the road). Follow this track past some houses to cross over the railway. Turn

Mapledurham House

The Thames at Pangbourne

right at a T-junction, now alongside some allotments on the left. Turn left along the road past Purley infant school. At the end of the road turn left along Mapledurham Drive (the Thames Path). Where the track bends left continue straight on along the left-hand edge of the field to Mapledurham Lock.

> To the right is a glimpse of Mapledurham House through the trees. It is owned by the Blount family and was named as Soames's house in John Galsworthy's *The Forsyte Saga*.

(**C**) At Mapledurham Lock turn left along the Thames Path back towards Pangbourne.

> An information board at Mapledurham Lock describes this peaceful stretch of the Thames as 'not having changed much since the sixteenth century'. Mapledurham Mill is visible across the lock on the other side of the river. Further on, Hardwick Hall is seen on the opposite bank. This impressive house may have been the

inspiration for Toad Hall in *The Wind in the Willows*, which Kenneth Graham wrote in Pangbourne. To complete the literary connections, it was at Pangbourne where Jerome K Jerome's *Three Men in a Boat* called it a day. At the end of this peaceful stretch is Pangbourne Meadows, owned by the National Trust. In the summer it is popular with people 'messing around in boats' or simply chilling out by the river. With Whitchurch Bridge as a backdrop it is a scene hardly changed since Edwardian times, which could have come straight out of a painting.

At the bridge turn left back to the car park. For the village hall and station continue straight along the road to the High Street then turn right. Turn right again at the T-junction.

9: Streatley

Streatley and Goring are two riverside villages at cross-roads both ancient and modern. In prehistoric times the Ridgeway and Icknield Way converged at the Thames here as this point was the safest crossing point for miles either side. Today the Ridgeway Path and Thames Path cross at this point (the traveller walking the Ridgeway Path leaves the North Wessex Downs and heads north-east along the Chiltern escarpment here). The walk leaves Streatley and climbs up onto the Downs via the Ridgeway path before heading south-east to the villages of Aldworth and Ashampstead. The climax of the walk is the ascent of Streatley Hill, rewarded with spectacular views across the Goring Gap.

Distance:	10½ miles/17km
Time:	3hr
Map:	OS Landranger 174/Explorer 158 and 170
Start:	Central car park in Goring (Grid Ref 600807)
Refreshments:	The Bell Inn, Aldworth; various pubs and cafés in Streatley and Goring

START: The central car park in Goring. The car park is pay-and-display. There is also limited free parking in a lay-by alongside a side road on the western edge of the village. Goring and Streatley Station (on the eastern side of the village) is on the Reading to Didcot line. There is additional parking at the station too. There is no obvious parking available in Streatley. Streatley is reached from Reading by proceeding west along the A329, then turning right along the B4009, crossing the river into Goring.

From the car park in Goring, turn left to reach the High Street, then left again down to the river, crossing into Streatley (and Berkshire).

Goring and Streatley are popular in the summer months with day trippers strolling down to the bridge to admire the view of Goring Lock and to walk along the towpath for a few yards. The bridge provides you with the best view of the two villages, with the wooded slopes of the Chilterns/Streatley Hill as a backdrop. At the main cross-roads in Streatley is the Bull Inn, an old coaching inn on the road between Reading and Oxford. There are various pubs in Goring, although as the walk is nearly 11 miles/18km long it is perhaps advisable to postpone sampling these hostelries until the end of the walk! St Mary's

Church, Streatley, has a fifteenth-century tower but the
rest of the church was rebuilt in the 1870s.

Goring Lock

Turn right along a track signposted 'The Thames Path'
passing to the right of the church. Fork left at a public
footpath sign, passing a recreation ground. Turn left
along a drive to reach the main road. Turn right along
this road, then left along Townsend Road, an unmade
road with some large houses. At the end turn left along
the A417 for a few paces, then sharp right along Rectory
Road, joining the Ridgeway Path.

Rectory Road is a long but quiet lane leading towards
the Downs. There is some local traffic, though, as there
are some isolated cottages further along the lane. After
passing the entrance to Goring and Streatley Golf Course
you get your first glimpse of the Downs.

Ignore two footpaths going off to the left. At Warren Farm
(the end of the bitumen) fork right, climbing steadily
towards open downland.

If you look back as you reach the top of the rise, there is a fine view across the Thames Valley back to the Chilterns.

(**A**) At the top of the rise turn left along a track. Follow the track round to the right, to reach a lane. Turn left

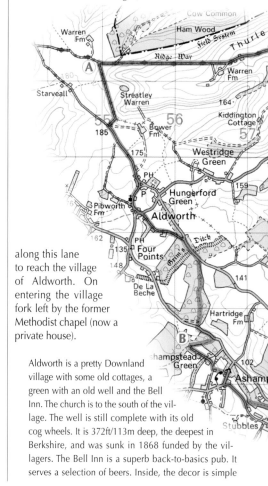

along this lane to reach the village of Aldworth. On entering the village fork left by the former Methodist chapel (now a private house).

Aldworth is a pretty Downland village with some old cottages, a green with an old well and the Bell Inn. The church is to the south of the village. The well is still complete with its old cog wheels. It is 372ft/113m deep, the deepest in Berkshire, and was sunk in 1868 funded by the villagers. The Bell Inn is a superb back-to-basics pub. It serves a selection of beers. Inside, the decor is simple but there is an open fire in winter and a 'No Smoking – You must be joking' sign. That scourge of modern living, the mobile phone, is thankfully banned here!

On leaving the pub, head south along the lane signposted to Compton and

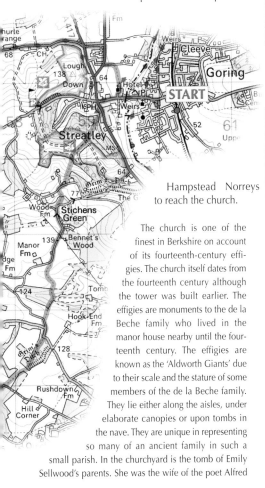

Hampstead Norreys to reach the church.

The church is one of the finest in Berkshire on account of its fourteenth-century effigies. The church itself dates from the fourteenth century although the tower was built earlier. The effigies are monuments to the de la Beche family who lived in the manor house nearby until the fourteenth century. The effigies are known as the 'Aldworth Giants' due to their scale and the stature of some members of the de la Beche family. They lie either along the aisles, under elaborate canopies or upon tombs in the nave. They are unique in representing so many of an ancient family in such a small parish. In the churchyard is the tomb of Emily Sellwood's parents. She was the wife of the poet Alfred

Aldworth church

Lord Tennyson. Tennyson loved the village so much he named his Sussex cottage after the place. The churchyard also contains an old yew tree, of which only the base remains after the rest of the tree was blown down in a gale in 1976. King Alfred is reputed to have made bows from its wood.

Fork left at a grass triangle to reach the B4009. Turn left along this road, then right along a by-way when the road bends left. At the end of this track turn right along a lane. At the end of the wood on the right (just before the road bends left) turn right along a track into the woods. Further on, continue straight on at a cross-tracks across a clearing. A yellow waymark post confirms you are on the right of way. Later the track bends round to the right. Turn left down some steps to reach a lane. Further on, turn right up a track into the woods. (**B**) Follow the track round to the left at the top of the rise (there is a cross-paths here). Ignore a public footpath sign on the right and continue straight on past some pretty cottages in the village of Ashampstead Green. Where the lane bends right, turn left by a public footpath sign.

A short detour, continuing straight on along the lane, will bring you to St Clement's Church. Inside are some thirteenth-century wall paintings showing the Annunciation, the Visitation (where an angel told Mary she was going to give birth to Jesus) and the Nativity (including the angels appearing to the shepherds).

Pass through the kissing gate and continue along the right-hand edge of a field. Turn right along a lane, then left at a T-junction. At a public footpath sign turn left into the woods. Turn right at a further public footpath sign along the top edge of the wood. The path later turns left and makes its way downhill to a lane. Turn right along this lane. (**C**) Turn left along a metalled track, climbing out of the valley. Continue straight on at the top of the rise. Where the track bends right turn left across the field to a waymark post. Follow the left-hand edge of the field for a few paces, then bear right across the field to the opposite side. Follow the right-hand edge of the field then cross the field to a wooden barrier at the entrance to a wood. Follow the path through the wood.

The earthwork alongside the path is Grim's Ditch. These were marked boundaries in Celtic times. The name Grim's Ditch is given to many such earthworks, which are associated with the Devil. These earthworks crop up all over the place in the nearby Chilterns.

On leaving the wood continue straight on along a lane. Where the lane bends left continue straight on along a smaller lane signposted to Southridge. Where this lane bends left turn right down the right-hand edge of the field to the wood ahead and on through the wood. Turn left by a public footpath sign in the dip. At the top, on leaving the wood, continue along the left-hand edge of the field to reach a lane. Turn right along this lane. Further on, the lane starts to descend. Ignore a by-way going off to the left. Where the lane bends right at the bottom bear left along a narrow path (by a public footpath sign). On leaving the trees turn left along the edge of the field to a lane in the valley bottom.

> The scene ahead is a tranquil English landscape, the houses in the valley complementing the view. Ahead, however, is Streatley Hill, the challenging finale to the walk. The way ahead is visible – going straight up the hill!

Turn right along this lane, then left by a public footpath sign, alongside a fence on your right. The path then bends right (still between fences) to a stile. Bear left over this stile, following the well-worn path up Streatley Hill. At the top continue straight on along the right-hand edge of the field and over at a cross-tracks.

The Goring Gap from Streatley Hill

> The top of Streatley Hill is owned by the National Trust as part of the Holies, an area of downland with walks and superb views. Along the top are some seats from

which to admire the spectacular views of the Goring Gap – the villages of Goring and Streatley alongside the Thames, sandwiched between the North Wessex Downs and the Chiltern Hills.

After admiring the view continue straight on downhill. It is a steep descent and a trekking pole may come in useful. At the bottom turn left along the A329. At the crossroads by the Bell Inn turn right along the B4009, down the main street of Streatley, back over the Thames into Goring, retracing your steps back to the start.

10: Stratfield Mortimer and the Devil's Highway

A gentle ramble across pastoral farmland with no steep climbs – ideal for a hot summer's day (also when the ground will be at its driest). The spire of Stratfield Mortimer church is a prominent landmark visible for much of the walk. The walk also takes in a stretch of the Devil's Highway, a Roman road between nearby Silchester and London.

Distance:	6½ miles/10.5km
Time:	2hr 30min
Map:	By Stratfield Mortimer church (Grid Ref 668672)
Start:	OS Landranger 175/Explorer 159
Refreshments:	The Fox and Horn, Stratfield Mortimer; The Old Elm Tree, Beech Hill

START: Stratfield Mortimer church. Stratfield Mortimer is reached from Reading by heading south along the A33 towards Basingstoke (leave the M4 at Junction 11). At the roundabout a few hundred yards south of the motorway turn right along a minor road to Grazeley, then on to Mortimer. The church is on the left just after the Fox and Horn pub. There is ample parking along the gravel drive to the church. Mortimer Station is to the south-west of the pub.

Facing the lych-gate turn left down to a bridge. Cross over a stile and turn right along a path between the field and a private garden. Further on, the path runs along the right-hand side of the field. Turn right over a footbridge, then turn left along the left-hand edge of the field alongside the Foudry Brook. Later turn left over a stile and bear left along the left-hand edge of the field. At the end of the second field turn left over two stiles along the right-hand edge of the next field. After crossing over the railway the path swings right across the field to a line of oak trees (there is a waymark arrow on the first tree). The trees, and later a hedge, are on the right-hand side of the path. (**A**) On reaching a lane turn left. At a T-junction continue straight on along the by-way opposite (the Devil's Highway).

Stratfield Mortimer church

The Devil's Highway is a Roman road which linked London with the nearby Roman town of Calleva Atrebatum, near Silchester. At this point it is the boundary between Berkshire and Hampshire. Further east the Devil's Highway crosses Finchampstead Ridges (Walk 4) and Bracknell Forest (Walk 3). In wet weather parts of the rutted track near the T-junction appear to be flooded, but it is still passable thanks to the 4x4 tracks.

Follow the Devil's Highway for about 1¼ miles/2km. It is a pleasant stroll between hedgerows. Further on, the path becomes gritted. After passing a cottage continue straight on along a minor road. (**B**) At a crossroads turn left.

Nearby is Stratfield Saye House, presented to the Duke of Wellington by the nation after he defeated Napoleon at Waterloo. In the grounds is the grave of Copenhagen, the horse he rode into battle.

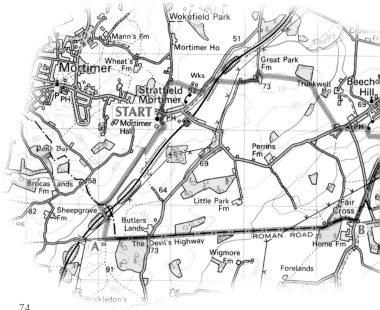

Looking back to Stratfield Mortimer

At a T-junction continue straight on along the track opposite past Great Hill's Farm. To the left are the houses of Beech Hill. After passing Cannon Bridge the track narrows to a path. (**C**) Turn left by a public footpath sign along the right-hand side of the field. At the end of the field turn right at a T-junction (hedge now on your left) and on through the woods to reach the village of Beech Hill. Turn right up the road to the Old Elm Tree pub. Turn left along Beech Hill Road.

Beech Hill is named after the de la Beche family who lived here before moving to Aldworth. They once owned a castle here, which has long since disappeared. Beside Beech Hill Road is a tablet marking the site of the Jubilee Reservoir built for the Diamond Jubilee of Queen Victoria. It provided the village with water until 1937 when a severe drought dried it up. The iron railings around the side were requisitioned for the war effort.

View across the fields from Beech Hill

Turn right along a path between cottages (by a public footpath sign). Continue straight on across three fields, to a bridlegate by a wood corner on the far side of the third field. Bear left through this bridlegate and alongside the wood edge. Where the fence bends right bear left across the field to a stile. Cross the next field to a further stile to the right of the farm buildings.

> To the right is a panoramic view across to the urban sprawl of Reading. The grand building ahead is Wokefield Park, now a conference and training centre.

After crossing a further stile pass along the left-hand edge of the next field, the farm buildings now on your left. Turn left through a gate along a drive between some barns and past the farmhouse. The drive then bends right. Further on, when the drive bends left, continue straight on over the stile. Bear left across the field, past the pylon on your left.

The farm that you have just walked through, Great Park Farm, was one of the farms given by Henry VIII as part of the marriage settlement to each of his wives. Ahead is the railway and the broach spire of Stratfield Mortimer church.

The path descends the hillside to a stile leading to the railway. Cross over the railway very carefully and the Foudry Brook to reach a road. Turn left along this road. Turn right by a public footpath sign along the right-hand side of the meadow. At the top of the rise bear left to a stile. Turn left along the road back to Stratfield Mortimer. At the T-junction in the village turn left. Where the road bends left turn right along the drive to the church and the start.

Stratfield Mortimer church was largely rebuilt in 1869 to include its landmark broach spire and two flying buttresses at the west end. Inside there is a Saxon tomb with an inscription referring to Aegelward (d.1017) who is mentioned in the Anglo-Saxon Chronicle.

11: Padworth

Starting from Padworth Common on the plateau above the Kennet Valley, there are fine views as you descend. After a tranquil stroll along the Kennet and Avon Canal, a gentle climb leads you to the pretty village of Ufton Nervet before returning to the fir trees and sandy heath of Padworth Common.

Distance:	7¾ miles/12.5km
Time:	3hr
Map:	OS Landranger 175/Explorer 159
Start:	Car park on Padworth Common (Grid Ref 619648)
Refreshments:	The Round Oak, Padworth Common

START: Padworth Common is reached from Reading by proceeding west along the A4, past Junction 12 of the M4. Just before the roundabout where the A340 branches off to the left, turn left along a minor road to Padworth. Go straight on over a crossroads in the village to reach the car park which is on the right just before the main road. Trains from Reading and Newbury stop at Aldermaston Wharf which is where the walk joins the Kennet and Avon Canal.

Padworth church

78

Turn left out of the car park, heading north along a quiet lane. Where the lane bends right, continue straight on along a drive (by a public footpath sign). After passing through a white gate the drive becomes a grassy track. At the end of this path turn left along a lane, then right along a track to Padworth church.

St John the Baptist Church, Padworth, is one of the most impressive Norman churches in the county. The building consists of an apsed chancel and a timber bell-turret. Both the north and south doorways include decorated colonnettes and arches.

Bear left along the path passing to the left of the church. Turn right along a drive, then left. Turn right along a track opposite the stables to a stile. Ahead is a fine view across the Kennet Valley. Continue straight on down the right-hand side of the paddock. Bear left across the next field to a footbridge by the opposite corner. Cross the next two fields via a stile, footbridge and further stile next to a waymark post. A path between fences leads across the River Kennet (past a waterfall) out to a track by an old mill. Turn left along this track to reach the A340. Turn right along this road, then right again along the canal towpath. (**A**)

The Kennet and Avon Canal was completed in 1810, providing an alternative to the notorious Bath Road for the transportation of goods from Bristol to London, the canal joining the Thames at Reading. It was the M4 of its day. However, the canal's success was short lived; the advent of the railways brought a decline in its fortunes as the leisurely pace of the canal (not to mention the water freezing over in winter and drought in summer) made it less attractive as a trade route. But Great Western Railways were obliged to maintain the canal under the Regulation of Railways Act. However, nationalisation in 1948 brought an end to this and the canal fell into disrepair and it was closed to navigation soon after. Since then the canal has been restored by the Kennet and Avon Canal Association/Trust and was reopened in 1990. The

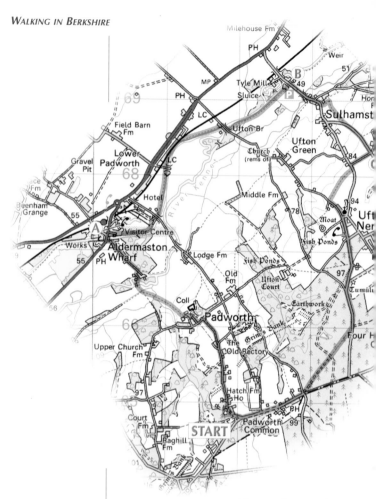

leisure age has given the canal a new lease of life. Today the canal gives pleasure to many people, be they walkers, cyclists, narrowboat cruisers or families on a day out. Near Aldermaston Wharf is the Kennet and Avon Canal Centre. Every Easter the canal forms part of the course for the Devizes to Westminster canoe race.

At Upton swing bridge the towpath crosses over to the southern bank. (**B**) At Tyle Mill Lock (there is further parking available here) turn right along the road. Ignore a public footpath sign right and Bottom Lane left, to begin the gentle climb out of the valley. Turn left over a stile at the top of the rise, along the left-hand edge of the field. On the far side of the field turn right (hedge still on the left) to rejoin the lane. Turn left along this lane to complete the climb. (**C**) Turn right along a path between fences at the top of the rise. To the right is another superb view across the Kennet Valley. When a lane is reached, continue straight on along the right-hand edge of the field opposite, then on along the left-hand edge of the next field. Turn left along the next lane to reach the pretty hamlet of Ufton Nervet.

Ufton Nervet church was built in 1862 in an early four-teenth-century style. It has a shingled spire. On the southern side of the churchyard is an ancient yew tree.

Continue straight on at a T-junction by the church (the main road comes in from the left), then straight on over a crossroads. Ignore two public footpath signs, left and right.

At this point the route crosses Grim's Bank (going off through the forest to the right). It is part of a boundary dyke, built in the fifth century by Britons living at nearby Silchester to keep out the invading Saxons!

Further on, bear right along a ride (past an Englefield Estate woodland notice), heedless of all turnings off.

The final stretch of the walk passes through some fine forest and heathland characteristic of the southern edge of the county (see also Walks 3 and 4). In the forest over to the left is Gibbet Piece. It was named after the hanging of two youths guilty of murder in 1787. The hanging attracted an audience of 10,000.

Padworth Common

On the far side of the forest, turn right along the road past the Round Oak pub. The car park is about half a mile along the road from the pub. Turn right along a minor road just before the main road bends left. The car park is on the left.

> Although it is at the end of the walk, the Round Oak pub offers a wide range of food and is an ideal place to relax at the end of the walk after you have changed out of your walking boots!

12: Bucklebury

Distance:	7½ miles/12km
Time:	3hr
Map:	OS Landranger 174/Explorer 159
Start:	Lay-by on Bucklebury Common (Grid Ref 556691)
Refreshments:	The Blade Bone Inn, Chapel Row; the Bull and the Old Boat, Stanford Dingley; the Pot Kiln, Frilsham

A peaceful walk through some remote countryside that is hidden from the A4. The scenery is varied, starting from the wooded Bucklebury Common, before descending to the Pang Valley and the pretty village of Stanford Dingley. A forest stretch brings you to the traditional Pot Kiln pub near Frilsham. The return is back down to the Pang Valley at Bucklebury village before climbing back to the common. It is not a steep climb – the biggest challenge is the mud (especially after rain)!

START: A small lay-by by the crossroads on Bucklebury Common where there is space for several cars. Bucklebury Common is reached from Reading by heading west along the A4 to Woolhampton (leave the M4 at Junction 12). Turn right at the western end of the village, climbing out of the Kennet Valley to Midgham Green. At a T-junction at the top turn left, bringing you to Bucklebury Common at the crossroads. The lay-by is over to the right. The nearest station is Midgham Station, in Woolhampton, adding about 4 miles/6.5km to the walk (but at least the return is downhill). From the eastern end of the lay-by bear left along a by-way. At a cross-tracks turn right. Follow the by-way along the top of the common, heedless of all turnings off. Follow a line of telegraph wires. At Chapel Row Cottage the track bears left to reach the village of Chapel Row.

Chapel Row is a 'scattered' village centred round the Blade Bone Inn. The bone that hangs from the pub is from a whale (found in the Kennet Valley?), although according to local folklore it was from a large beast that terrorised the village until the locals trapped and killed it. The village's other landmark is the avenue of oaks along the road to Bradfield (to the east of the village). The avenue was first planted in 1568 when Elizabeth I visited

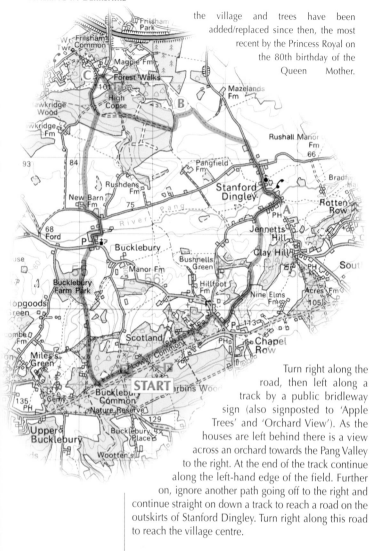

the village and trees have been added/replaced since then, the most recent by the Princess Royal on the 80th birthday of the Queen Mother.

Turn right along the road, then left along a track by a public bridleway sign (also signposted to 'Apple Trees' and 'Orchard View'). As the houses are left behind there is a view across an orchard towards the Pang Valley to the right. At the end of the track continue along the left-hand edge of the field. Further on, ignore another path going off to the right and continue straight on down a track to reach a road on the outskirts of Stanford Dingley. Turn right along this road to reach the village centre.

Stanford Dingley is one of those 'picture postcard' villages,

Orchard near Chapel Row

full of attractive cottages with the River Pang flowing through the middle. There are also a couple of pubs although, unless you made a late start, it is too soon into the walk to stop for lunch! Save one of them for a relaxing drink/meal afterwards.

(**A**) Turn left at the T-junction in the village, past the cottages and houses, crossing the River Pang to reach the church at the northern end of the village.

The Church of St Denys was restored in 1885 although the original church dates from the twelfth century. It has a weatherboarded bell-turret. In the churchyard there are some Spanish chestnut trees and an urn (on a pedestal) in memory of Richard Carter (d.1773). Entry to the churchyard is by a war memorial lych-gate beside which there is a small sun-dial.

Continue straight on past the church, ignoring paths going off to the left and right. At the top of the rise (after passing roads left and right) turn left over a stile along the left-hand edge of the fields. There is an electric fence separating you from the cows! When a track comes in from the right bear left along a track between fences. (**B**) At a yellow waymark turn left over a stile along the left-hand side of the field. On the far side of the field turn left along a track inside a strip of woodland. Turn right along a wide track between the forest and a young plantation, climbing at first. At the top of the rise turn right at a cross-paths (by a public footpath sign). Fork left immediately. On leaving the wood continue along the right-hand edge of the field ahead to reach the lane.

In the spring the wood on your right is covered in blue-bells. This is a beautiful, remote spot despite the drone of the traffic on the M4 only half a mile from here.

Turn left along this lane to reach the Pot Kiln pub.

The Pot Kiln is a wonderful old-fashioned pub with basic decor but with a garden overlooking the woods and fields. The pub brews its own beer and has a varied menu – though, in the middle of a walk, the puddings are best left alone! The small hallway leading to the bar has an old photograph of some vintage Austin cars outside the pub, below which is a parody of Psalm 23 (the shepherd becoming an Austin!).

Stanford Dingley

Stanford Dingley church

The Pot Kiln, Frilsham

(**C**) Continue straight on along the road past the pub. Where the lane bends right at the top of the rise continue straight on along a track into the woods. Continue straight on when this track bends left. When this second track bends left turn right down a narrow path through the woods. There are intermittent waymark arrows on trees to guide you. On leaving the wood continue straight on across two fields via a stile. The path is usually well defined. In the third field bear left to a stile. Take the right fork through some trees and continue straight on down the right-hand side of a large field. At the bottom, cross over a farm drive across a paddock to reach a lane. Turn left along this lane, following it round towards Bucklebury. Where the lane bends right continue straight on through a kissing gate and across a meadow to reach the churchyard. Bear right, passing the church on your left to reach another lane.

The church (St Mary's) is of Norman origin and includes an ornate south doorway, which contains rosettes and flowers. In the centre is a face with a crown and orb. This may be surprising but in the past this peaceful village was regarded as the capital of the Pang Valley. Reading

Abbey built a house for the abbot here, which was sold to the Winchcombe family on the dissolution of the monasteries.

On leaving the churchyard continue straight on along the lane. Turn left by a public bridleway sign after the last cottage. This later becomes a sunken track and starts the longish climb back to Bucklebury Common. At the top of the first rise follow the track through the woods as it levels out for a while. Ignore a path going off to the right. Near the top of the second rise continue straight on along a drive, ignoring two cross-paths. By a cottage garden with a thatched shed (the cottage itself is out of sight) fork left along a by-way (indicated by a red waymark arrow). Turn left at a cross-tracks. Further on, this track becomes concrete. On reaching a lane turn right back to the start.

13: Donnington Castle

Starting from Snelsmore Common Country Park, an area of heathland and woodland, the route crosses pastoral farmland via the pretty village of Winterbourne to a ridge leading to the village of Bagnor. The climax of the walk is Donnington Castle, still bearing the scars of the Civil War.

Distance:	6¾ miles/10.5km
Time:	2hr 45min
Map:	OS Landranger 174/Explorer 158
Start:	Entrance to Snelsmore Common Country Park (Grid Ref 463711)
Refreshments:	The Blackbird, Bagnor

START: The car park at Snelsmore Common Country Park. This is reached from Newbury by proceeding north from the roundabout at Speen (the A4) along the B4494. The entrance to the car park is about half a mile on the left after crossing the Newbury by-pass. From the other direction leave the M4 at Junction 13 (A34 turn) and

Cottage at Winterbourne

head south towards
Newbury. Turn off the
dual carriageway after
about a mile (the first exit),
then turn right at two T-junc-
tions before and after crossing
the A34. Turn left along a minor
road to reach the B4494. Turn left
along this road. The entrance to the park is on
the right after passing another minor road. There are
public toilets at the entrance.

From the car park take the path through the woods,
passing to the right of a picnic place to reach a road.
Turn left along this road. At the end of the woods bear
right through a squeeze stile (opposite a large house,
Winterbourne Holt) and take the path along the left-
hand edge of the field (parallel to the road). The path
then swings right to a public footpath sign and kissing
gate. Cross the next field to a kissing gate in the opposite fence and continue along the right-hand edge of
this third field to reach a lane. Turn right along this
lane, passing a picturesque thatched cottage with a
stream running through its garden. Turn left along a

91

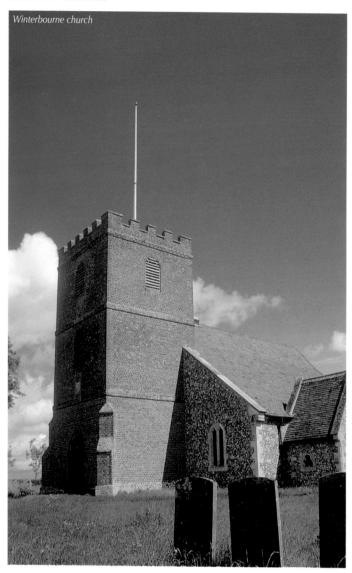

Winterbourne church

path, passing to the right of this cottage (the path gets a bit overgrown in the summer), and continue along the left-hand edge of the field. Near the top of the rise bear left through a gate and continue along the right-hand edge of the next field. To the left is a fine view across the Lambourn Valley to Newbury. At a lane turn left, then right along a track between Winterbourne Manor and church.

> Winterbourne Manor and church are set on a hilltop overlooking the village itself, which is in a dry chalk valley below. The manor is a red-brick Georgian building. The church dates from the twelfth century but was rebuilt with its brick tower and battlements in the eighteenth century. The North Chapel dates from the time of the rebuilding. A few parts of the original church remain, notably a couple of windows in the chancel.

The track passes between some farm buildings and crosses a larger field towards Lower Farm, ahead. Just before the farm the track veers to the right. Turn left at a cross-tracks, heedless of all turnings off. Near the top of the rise turn right through a bridlegate, along the right-hand edge of the field. (**A**) At a gate in the field corner turn left, eventually leading to a lane. Turn right along this lane. Near the top of the rise turn left over a stile by a public footpath sign. Follow the waymarked path through the wood. Further on, fork right at a waymark post. On leaving the wood cross the field to a stile and continue straight down the middle of the second field to a stile in the opposite fence.

> The wood you have just walked through forms part of Boxford Common, which was once an Iron Age settlement. The fields are a tranquil spot, the tranquillity emphasised by the woods that surround these two fields.

The path carries on down through the woods. On leaving the woods continue straight on over a cross-tracks, bearing slightly right (hedge on left). The path now follows the long ridge down towards Bagnor. All around are views across open country, to Newbury on the right and Snelsmore Common on the left. As the path descends from the ridge a metalled track comes in from the right. Further on, the track swings left (joining the Lambourn Valley Way) to reach the village of Bagnor. Turn right along a lane through the village.

> Bagnor is a pretty village alongside the River Lambourn. Its highlights are the Blackbird pub and the Watermill Theatre. The pub (which can get busy on a Sunday lunchtime) offers an extensive range of bar meals and beers and is ideal for a stop before the final stretch. On the other side of the road is the old mill. There has been a mill here since Domesday times, producing among other things quality writing paper. Today the building has been converted into a theatre. A number of major (and varied) productions are put on here each year (box office tel 01635 46044).

(**B**) Fork left along a track signposted to Donnington – an extension of the Lambourn Valley Way at the pub. Cross over the A34. Where the track bends right along the top edge of the golf course continue straight on, then turn right along the inside edge of the wood. This path leads to the entrance to Donnington Castle. (**C**) Turn left through a kissing gate up to the gatehouse.

> Although only the gatehouse remains (the rest of the castle was demolished after the Civil War) this is the only castle in Berkshire (apart from Windsor, of course) which has more than earthworks to show. Richard II granted a licence to build the castle in 1386 and it was held by the Crown on and off until the Civil War. Colonel John Boys took command of the castle on behalf of the king in September 1643. The castle was attacked several times by the Parliamentary forces without success in 1644 and 1645.

On the far side of the castle turn left along a track. After some farm buildings the track swings left to cross the A34. The new track then turns right (parallel to the road)

Donnington Castle

back to the top of the rise, then swings left (to rejoin the old track). Where the track forks take the right fork, leading back to the woods of Snelsmore Common.

> Snelsmore Common is an extensive area of heathland and woodland which has been turned into a country park. It is ideal for dog walking and there are various picnic areas as well for family days out.

Follow this track, heedless of all turnings off, across the common. Further on, when this track bends left, continue straight on across an area of heathland (a marker post directs you back towards the car park). At a T-junction turn right, then left back to the start.

14: The Ridgeway

Distance:	13½ miles/22km
Time:	6hr
Map:	OS Landranger 174/Explorer 158 and 170
Start:	Car park on Bury Down (Grid Ref 479840)
Refreshments:	The Fox and Hounds, Peasemore

An introduction to the North Wessex Downs, starting from Bury Down on the Ridgeway, one of England's oldest roads. Much of the route is over downland tracks, making for easy walking with plenty of wide views. The walk also visits the village of Peasemore.

START: The car park at Bury Down on the Ridgeway. It is reached from Newbury by travelling north on the A34 (Junction 13 of the M4), then leaving the dual carriageway along a minor road signposted to West Ilsley. Turn right in the village up another minor road signposted to Chilton (opposite the church). The car park is about a mile up on the Downs where the road crosses the Ridgeway. From Reading and Oxford take the A329 to Streatley, then turn left along the B4009 for a superb ride across the Downs. Turn right along a minor road by the Four Points pub to Compton and on to West/East Ilsley.

From the car park head east along the Ridgeway. Turn right by a public bridleway sign along the right-hand edge of a series of fields (ignore a bridleway going off to the right). At the end of the third field bear left along a track to reach the eastern edge of West Ilsley. Turn right along the road for a few paces, then bear left along a drive past the former Baptist chapel (now converted to a house). Follow the drive round to the left towards Hodcott House.

Hodcott House was built as a home for a racehorse trainer, with some stables attached. The Downs are classic racehorse country. Alongside the Ridgeway are some 'gallops' where the horses are put through their paces. The early 1990s TV drama series *Trainer* was filmed around here.

98

Further on, the track bends right, passing to the right of Hodcott House. On the far side of the house bear left, gently climbing up onto the Downs. Ignore a public footpath going off to the right. At the top of the rise the track bends right. To the left is a fine view across the Downs. Further on, turn left at a T-junction to reach a by-way. Turn right along this by-way, heedless of all turnings off. After passing a couple of barns on the right and a radio/TV mast in the middle of the field on your left, a further by-way is passed going off to the left.

Soon another by-way comes in from the right. Eventually a road is reached. Turn right along this road for a few paces, then left along a minor road to reach the village of Peasemore. In the village turn right at a T-junction, then left along a path opposite Mell Green. Further on, follow the left-hand edge of a paddock, then continue along a drive to reach a lane by the cricket field. Turn left along this lane, then left again at a T-junction to reach the Fox and Hounds pub.

The Fox and Hounds is the only pub on the route, although it is closed on Mondays (except bank holidays). The pub offers a wide range of bar food with some tempting puddings, but remember there are still three

Peasemore

*View across to
East Ilsley*

hours (8–9 miles/13–14.5km) of walking to do! A nice touch are the seats in the porch to ease the removal (and lacing-up) of boots.

(**A**) Turn right along a track by a public footpath sign just after the pub. Where the track bends right bear left through a squeeze stile across the field towards the church, leading out to a lane. Turn left along this lane.

The medieval church has eighteenth-century additions, including the tower, spire and bell, funded by 'William Coward, Gentleman'. He also provided for the poor of the parish in his will when he died in 1739. Peasemore itself is a large village with a variety of buildings set high up on the Downs. The author Miss Read was the schoolmistress here for a short while in the early 1950s, teaching a single class of sixteen 5 to 11 year olds. In a personal feature in *The AA Book of British Villages* (1980) she fondly recalls her time at the school, teaching in idyllic surroundings – the hymns being played on the old Victorian piano; nature walks around the village, stopping to chat with mothers in cottage gardens and farmers in the fields; and lunchtime patrol in the play-ground out in the exhilarating downland air. Sadly falling numbers meant that the school was to close a few years later, and it is now a private house.

Continue straight on past the church along the lane sign-posted to Chievelly and Downland. Where the lane bends right bear left over a step stile in the wall. Cross the field to a gate in the opposite fence, to the left of the barns. Continue straight on down the track. Where the track bends left continue straight on along by a hedge on your right to a by-way at the bottom. Cross over this by-way and bear slightly right across the large field opposite. The path is usually well defined, if somewhat faint. On the far side of the field turn left along a track (ignore the public footpath). Continue straight on at the top of the rise. Where the track bends left, carry straight on down a path to reach Beedon.

In the village turn right, then left. At the bottom bear right along a concrete track to pass underneath the A34. Near the top of the rise turn right along a concrete track by a public bridleway sign. Further on, this path runs along the bottom edge of a large meadow. Continue straight on at a cross-paths (the path going off to the left peters out after passing through the scrub). (**B**) Turn left at a cross-tracks in a belt of trees. At a T-junction turn left for the long climb up to Shrill Down. The path is wholly within the trees, although there are glimpses of the Downs from time to time. Eventually turn right at a T-junction.

In the valley bottom is East Ilsley, an attractive village built below the knoll on which the church stands, around a large duckpond. This knoll has been holy ground since before the advent of Christianity. Once a sacred thorn tree grew there, which was the site of Druidic rites. Today the village is associated with the training of racehorses, although it was once famous for its sheep fairs. The then Lord of the Manor, Sir Francis Moore, received a charter for a sheep and corn market in 1620 which attracted farmers from all over southern England, travelling across the Downs. At the height of these fairs there were thirteen pubs in the village. The

Track leading to East Ilsley

sheep fairs ended in the 1930s. There is a mural depicting the sheep fairs in the tunnel where the Ridgeway passes underneath the A34.

At the bottom continue straight on over the lane for the final climb back to the Ridgeway. Continue straight on over a cross-tracks near the top of the rise. (**C**) At the top turn left along the Ridgeway.

The Ridgeway is said to be one of the oldest roads in Europe and this section across the crest of the Downs was originally a drovers' route. The tracks naturally followed the high ground, avoiding the wooded and boggy ground in the valleys. It was first used in the Bronze Age (there is no evidence of its use before then) as part of a route from the Channel at Lyme Regis in Dorset to the Wash at Hunstanton in Norfolk. The Ridgeway Path, opened in 1973, follows the Wessex Downs from Overton Hill (near Avebury) to Streatley, then along the Chiltern Escarpment to Ivinghoe Beacon (85 miles/137km in all). This part of the Ridgeway is popular with walkers, horseriders, mountain bikers (and unfortunately trail bikers). To the north are superb views across the Vale of the White Horse (Wittenham Clumps near Wallingford can be seen).

The Ridgeway gently climbs to the summit of Several Down.

There is a welcome drinking water tap on your left to refresh you for the final stretch. Alongside the path are some 'gallops' where the racehorses are put through their paces.

Further on, the path passes beneath the A34. In the tunnel are some murals, one depicting the East Ilsley sheep fairs. Soon a bridleway goes off to the left, then the bridleway down to West Ilsley, taken at the start of the walk, is reached. A little further on is the car park on Bury Down.

15: Downland Villages

A tour of some pretty villages, set among the majestic landscape of the Downs. The villages are all in remote locations, linked by quiet lanes and ancient tracks in scenery that is forever England. It is a long walk but there are no steep climbs, just easy-going tracks across undulating countryside.

The Old Rectory, Farnborough

Distance:	11½ miles/19km
Time:	5hr
Map:	OS Landranger 174/Explorer 158 and 170
Start:	By the church in Farnborough (Grid Ref 436819)
Refreshments:	The Stag, Leckhampstead; The Ibex, Chaddleworth

START: Farnborough, 2½ miles (4km) west of West Ilsley. To reach Farnborough follow the directions to West Ilsley (see Walk 14) but continue straight on along the lane through the village, past the cricket pitch and the Harrow Inn. Farnborough is the next village along the way. There is a small parking area in the village, east of the church. There is further parking where the lane from

West Ilsley joins the by-way east of Farnborough (Grid Ref 453812).

Cottage in Peasemore

> Farnborough is one of the highest villages in Berkshire, set high up on the Downs. It was a stopping point on the old packhorse track which crossed the chalk downlands between Hungerford and Oxford. The church, which overlooks the Downs, is of Norman origin but with a fifteenth-century tower. Inside there is a window designed by John Piper in memory of Sir John Betjeman who lived at the Rectory for a few years from 1945. The Rectory is Farnborough's finest building, built in 1749 in the Dutch style.

From the church head east along the road past the Rectory. When the road bends left continue straight on along a track past some farm buildings. Bear left across the fields on a well-defined public footpath (ignore the very muddy track going off to the right through the trees). To the left is a superb view across the Downs to the Ridgeway and Bury Down. (**A**) On the far side of the field pass through some scrub and turn right along a by-way. Continue straight on along a lane (there is further parking available here). Where the lane bends right continue straight on along a track between fields leading to a T-junction (the last section can be a bit muddy). Turn left here. Ignore a footpath going off to the right. Further on, another by-way comes in from the left. When a lane is reached continue straight on. The track later descends gently.

(**B**) Turn right at a cross-paths (hedge on left), leading to a track. Where this track bends left at the top of the rise (by a barn on the left) bear left across the meadow to a step stile in the opposite wall, leading to a lane on the outskirts of Peasemore. Continue along this lane to reach the church.

Peasemore church was rebuilt in the Perpendicular style in 1842 to include a spire, which has become a landmark all around. The tower was built in red brick in 1737, funded by 'William Coward, Gentleman'.

Continue straight on past the church, along the lane signposted to Leckhampstead. Turn left by a public footpath sign, passing to the right of the church. Bear right across a (!) garden to a waymark post and on across a large field to reach a lane. Here turn left, then right to cross a further field in the same direction as before to reach another lane. Turn right along this lane. At a T-junction continue straight on along a by-way which follows the right-hand side of the green at first, before it bears right along a track between fields. Further on, it swings left to reach the B4494 in the valley bottom. Cross over the B4494 and continue straight on up the lane to Leckhampstead.

Leckhampstead is a scattered village centred around a triangular village green. Alongside the green to the south is the Stag pub and on the green itself is an unusual war memorial obelisk incorporating a clock.

Leckhampstead Green

The cottages are a mix of traditional thatch and modern council designs. On the way to Chaddleworth (Leckhampstead Thicket) is a small red-brick Methodist chapel built in 1874.

At the village green turn right along the road signposted to Chaddleworth, past the Methodist chapel. Continue straight on at a crossroads (past a tiny village shop). At the T-junction by the school turn left to reach the Ibex pub.

Chaddleworth is the largest (and arguably the most attractive) village on the tour. The main 'street' of cottages is the road leading from just south of the pub up to the church. The church, which is at the top of the hill overlooking the village, is Early English but with some Norman features. If you can last out that long (there are also pubs in Leckhampstead and Peasemore – albeit with a short detour) the Ibex pub is recommended for a lunchtime break (about 2hr 30min walking from the start). There is a conservatory and beer garden at the back.

(**C**) Turn right along the passageway opposite the pub. Turn right along the main lane through the village. At a public footpath sign turn right, crossing a field to reach another lane just past a children's playground. (For the church continue straight on up the lane.) Continue straight on across this lane (past a pretty pink thatched cottage) along the right-hand edge of the field.

> Over to the left is Chaddleworth House, built in 1830 within a small park.

Turn right over a stile between a fence and hedge, then straight on between fields to reach a lane. Turn left along this lane. When the lane bends right continue straight on along the left-hand side of the field, alongside Spray Wood on the left. At the end of the wood continue straight on across the field towards Brightwalton ahead (the spire of All Saints Church is a landmark). Turn left along the lane signposted to Farnborough. By the war memorial turn right along the lane past the church.

> The church, along with the nearby school and Rectory, was built in 1862–63 by G E Street. It is in thirteenth-century style. The shingled spire and south aisle was described in *Murray's Berkshire Architectural Guide* (edited by John Betjeman and John Piper) as 'one of Street's happiest designs'. He rebuilt or restored many of the parish churches in both Berkshire and neighbouring Buckinghamshire in Victorian times. The Rectory is an individual design featuring brick chimney stacks which run down the length of the building. Elsewhere the village contains several brick and cob cottages, some with thatched roofs.

Turn left by a public footpath sign opposite a public phone booth and postbox. Bear right across the meadow to a stile in the opposite corner and continue along the right-hand edge of a paddock to reach a lane. Turn right along this lane. At a T-junction turn left along a track. When the track forks take the left fork, climbing gently.

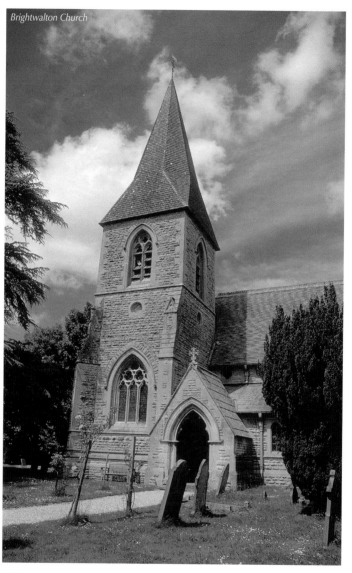

Brightwalton Church

At the top is a panoramic view across the Downs, with Farnborough church ahead.

Turn right along the lane, along the ridge top, to reach the B4494. Turn right along this road. There is a wide verge! At a public footpath sign turn left down the field. In the dip the path swings left and follows a line of telegraph poles to reach a lane leading to Farnborough. Turn right over a stile (in the undergrowth) opposite a drive coming in from the left. Cross the paddock to a stile (in the direction of the right hand of the two public footpath signs). Continue along the top edge of a large field (fence on your left). To the right is a wide view across the Downs. Turn left over a stile and bear left across the paddock via a series of gates and stiles to reach a stile by the church. This leads out to the lane and parking area at the start of the walk.

16: Lambourn Downs (East)

Ah, the Lambourn Downs – the sense of freedom experienced when walking along well-defined tracks across the wide open spaces of the Downs. There are fine views all around before descending to the pretty village of East Garston. A stretch of the old Lambourn Valley Line brings you to Eastbury before returning to Lambourn across the Downs to the south of the valley.

Distance:	10 miles/16km
Time:	5hr
Map:	OS Landranger 174/Explorer 158
Start:	Free car park in Lambourn (Grid Ref 325787)
Refreshments:	The village shop in East Garston; The Plough, Eastbury; various pubs and cafés (and a fish and chip shop) in Lambourn

START: The free car park in Lambourn. Lambourn is reached by leaving the M4 at Junction 14, then proceeding along the A338 towards Wantage. After about a quarter of a mile turn left onto the B4000 which descends into the town. The car park is on the left down the High Street (now the B4001). Alternatively, leave Wantage (A417/A338) by taking the B4507 west (towards Whitehorse Hill). At a crossroads turn left onto the B4001 for a superb ride across the Downs, to approach Lambourn from the north.

The Thamesdown bus service between Swindon and Newbury stops in the market square in Lambourn.

Turn left out of the car park. At the crossroads in the town centre continue straight on along Market Place, past the church.

Lambourn is a small but thriving market town in a valley high up on the Downs. The Lambourn Valley is known as 'The Valley of the Racehorse'. Much of the town is dependent on horseracing – there are several stables nearby. The High Street has some individual shops as well as several pubs. The town was granted a market in the Middle Ages and the Market Cross stands in front of the church. Before the advent of horseracing, sheep were the main 'industry' of the town. The church is one of the

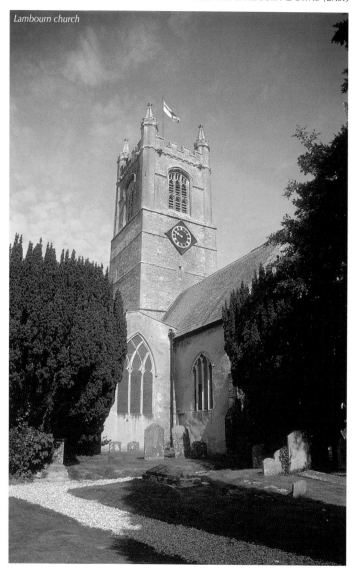

Lambourn church

finest in Berkshire, originally a late Norman cruciform building. Transepts, three chapels and the large tower were later added. The tower has become a landmark from all around.

On the outskirts of the village bear right along Sheepdrove Road (past a sign for Sheepdrove Organic Farm/Warren Farm) to climb out of the valley. Looking back there is a superb view of Lambourn. Fork right opposite Highfield House. The lane descends into a dip before climbing up the other side. Near the top of the rise continue straight on over a cross-tracks. At the top of

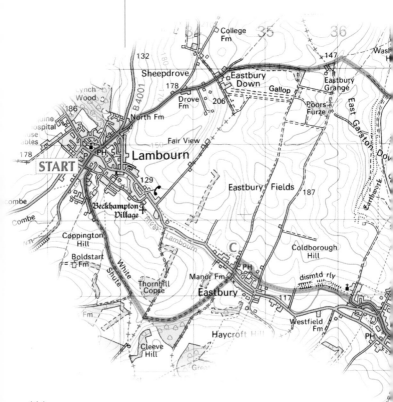

the rise the bitumen ends and the way becomes a rough track. Where the track forks take the right fork, soon descending. Ahead is a panoramic view across the Downs. Continue straight on over a by-way at the bottom. When the track forks turn right uphill, heedless of all turnings off. The track climbs up to Pound's Farm.

> Near the top of the rise is a 'gallops' where the race-horses are put through their paces. Unfortunately the view to the right across East Garston Down is somewhat marred by a pig farm!

At the top of the rise continue straight on along the lane past Pound's Farm. (**A**) Follow the lane round to the right. Just before the lane starts to descend turn left along a by-way, which then swings right to follow the right-hand edge of a large field. Ignore a cross-paths. Further on, the path bends left to pass around the outside edge of a spinney. Ignore a footpath going off to the left and a permissive track (not an official right of way) going off to the right. (**B**) At the bottom turn right along the Lambourn Valley Way, after passing the buildings of Maidencourt Farm. The path crosses a meadow parallel to the River Lambourn to reach a kissing gate, then follows the left-hand edge of a large field to reach the village of East Garston. Continue straight on along a track, then a lane through the village.

> East Garston is a 'picture postcard' English village with its rows of pretty black-timbered and white-washed cottages, some with thatched roofs, along the main street. The River Lambourn flows through the village and

115

Pound's Farm

The course of the Lambourn Valley Line

some of the cottages have their own bridges across the river. The village has a general stores with a small village green (with a bench) by the river nearby.

At the end of the village the road bends right towards the church (All Saints). Turn left along a path between fences just before the church (still on the Lambourn Valley Way).

This stretch of the walk follows the course of the old Lambourn Valley Line, a branch line of the Great Western Railway from Lambourn, along the valley to Newbury, which fell foul of Dr Beecham and his (not so merry!) band of accountants in the 1960s.

All Saints Church is a Norman cruciform church – a smaller version of the one at Lambourn. Like many other churches it was restored in Victorian times.

Further on, turn left up some steps and turn right along the right-hand side of a field to reach a kissing gate. Cross over a track and bear slightly right along a track between fences. This path becomes overgrown in summer but is still passable. Continue straight on over a lane (via some steps). Turn left down a track at a cross-paths to reach a lane. Turn left along this lane to reach the Plough Inn in the heart of Eastbury.

> The Plough Inn is rightly popular with walkers and locals. This homely pub is well worth the wait (it is about three-quarters of the way round). Inside it has a horseracing theme. There is a large variety of bar meals on offer. The pub sign is unusual – a painting of the pub at night with the Plough constellation in the sky above. Near the pub is the small Victorian church, designed by G E Street in 1853. The church itself is unremarkable apart from a window in the south wall, engraved by Laurence Whistler in memory of the poet Edward Thomas, who lived locally and is buried alongside his wife in the churchyard here.

(**C**) On leaving the pub take the track opposite, past Spills Farm. Follow the track round to the right (ignoring a public footpath sign). Looking back there is a fine view of Eastbury, with the Downs as a backdrop. Where the

The Plough, Eastbury

track forks at the top of the rise take the right fork which swings round to the right between a wood and a field. At a T-junction bear right across the field in the direction of a public footpath sign to reach a stile in the opposite fence. Make for just to the right of the dip ahead. Turn right along a track, heedless of all turnings off.

> This is the White Shute, the old road from Lambourn to Hungerford. On the right is the Wates Nature Reserve, a piece of unspoilt downland with many wild flowers, in the summer resembling an alpine meadow. It is now a Site of Special Scientific Interest. Along the path is a stile granting access to the reserve with a noticeboard with information about the site. At the top of the rise is a view across to Lambourn with the church tower acting as a landmark.

Follow the lane to the right after passing Lambourn primary school. Turn left at a T-junction to return to the High Street. Turn right, back to the car park and market square.

17: Lambourn Downs (West)

Distance:	10 miles/16km
Time:	5hr
Map:	OS Landranger 174/Explorer 158 and 170
Start:	Free car park in Lambourn (Grid Ref 325787)
Refreshments:	The Malt Shovel, Upper Lambourn; various pubs, cafés and a fish and chip shop in Lambourn

A word of advice about the weather. Unlike the sheltered woods and valleys, the Downs can be wild and bleak so it is advisable to save walks across the Downs for a dry day – the wide open spaces provide precious little shelter from a heavy shower!

START: Free car park off the High Street in Lambourn. See Walk 16.

Turn left out of the car park down the High Street to the Market Square. Turn left along a footpath between

The Lambourn Downs is characterised by its well-defined tracks and wide views to the west of the village. The gallops, where the racehorses are put through their paces, are more evident on this walk, although the Lambourn Valley's image as 'The Valley of the Racehorse' is well publicised on the approach. Ashdown House is glimpsed through the trees on the first part of the walk. Later the route passes by the Seven Barrows, now a nature reserve. The return to Lambourn is via Upper Lambourn with its pretty thatched cottages and the Malt Shovel pub.

View across the Downs

Lambourn Almshouses

the church and almshouses (past the estate agent). This is
the Lambourn Valley Way.

> The large church is one of the finest in Berkshire. Its
> prominent crossing tower is a landmark from all around.
> It is the work of an architect influenced by the Cotswold
> or West Country traditions. The almshouses on your right
> were rebuilt in 1852 by T Talbot Bury; the castellated
> facade leads to a small cloisters.

At the end of the path continue straight on along the
road. Turn left up Folly Road, passing some large houses
and Hill House Stables as you climb up to the Downs.
Fork right at the end of the bitumen. (**A**) Turn right at a
cross-tracks.

> Over to the right are some training gallops – you are
> more likely to meet horses rather than fellow walkers on
> these tracks.

Where the track bends left, continue straight on across
the Downs in the direction of a by-way sign. Bear left –
there is a faint track to guide you – to a gate leading to a
further track.

Ahead is Ashdown House, a Dutch-style seventeenth-century house. The Earls of Craven lived here in the eighteenth century and started horseracing here when they realised that the Downs were ideal for training horses. It was from this point on that

Seven Barrows

Lambourn became a centre for horse-racing, which soon surpassed sheep as the town's main source of income. Ashdown House is now owned by the National Trust and is open on Wednesday and Saturday afternoons from April to October. Inside there is a grand staircase which leads to the roof, from which there are superb views across the Downs and the formal parterre gardens in front of the house.

Continue straight on over a cross-tracks to reach the B4000. Ashdown House is about a mile along the road to the north. (**B**) Cross over the road and bear right up the track opposite. Ignore a bridleway going off to the right and a footpath off to the left at the top of the rise. Continue straight on over a cross-paths in the dip. The track then swings left, then right to pass along the outside edge of a spinney, then on up towards Well-bottom Down. (**C**) Turn right at a T-junction at the top of the rise. Turn left along a bridleway (fence on your left). On the right are some more 'gallops' and over to the left is a fine panoramic view across to the Ridgeway between Waylands Smithy and Whitehorse Hill. At the bottom the track swings right. Turn left along a track, leading up to a road.

By the side of the road is a small metal bollard marking the county boundary between Berkshire and Oxfordshire. Before 1974 the whole of the Lambourn Downs (including Whitehorse Hill and Waylands Smithy) were in Berkshire.

Turn right along this road, past Seven Barrows House.

The Seven Barrows (although there are more than that!) is a group of round barrows dating from the Bronze Age (1800–500 BC). The group includes a bell, bowl and a disc barrow. There are also two twin barrows (two smaller mounds surrounded by one ditch). The area is now a nature reserve where some species of butterfly and small mammals can be seen as well as many downland plants, as the grasslands surrounding the barrows have never been ploughed.

(**D**) Follow the road round to the right at the nature reserve. Where the lane bends left continue straight on along a by-way. At the top of the rise a track comes in from the right. Carry straight on over a cross-tracks to reach the hamlet of Upper Lambourn. (**E**) At the bottom

Seven Barrows

125

Fulke Walwyn Way

turn left at a T-junction, the Fulke Walwyn Way, and on past some pretty cottages.

Upper Lambourn is a linear settlement along a single lane among the stables. The Fulke Walwyn Way is named after one of Lambourn's most successful trainers. His long list of successes includes a Grand National win and four Cheltenham Gold Cups. The path is a 'dual carriageway' with separate paths for walkers and riders on either side of a ditch.

At the end of the village road is the Malt Shovel pub, which is popular with everyone involved in horseracing from stable lads and lasses to trainers as well as walkers and cyclists. Inside there are pictures of racing scenes and winners from over the years. The bar offers a selection of ales including Archers, brewed locally in Swindon, together with a range of food. It is well worth the wait, being near the end of the walk.

Bear left along a path between fences opposite the pub to reach the B4000. Turn left along this road, passing the Equine Hospital on the right, then Folly Road. Retrace your steps back into Lambourn.

18: Kintbury and Hungerford

Distance:	7¾ miles/12.5km
Time:	3hr
Map:	OS Landranger 174/Explorer 158
Start:	Car park opposite Kintbury Station (Grid Ref 385673)
Refreshments:	The Three Swans Hotel and various pubs, cafés and shops in Hungerford; The Dundas Arms, Kintbury

A gentle walk, this. The first part crosses softly undulating farmland towards Hungerford (with a view across to Walbury Hill) before returning along the Kennet and Avon Canal.

START: The car park on the other side of the road to Kintbury Station. Kintbury is reached by leaving the M4 at Junction 13 (the Newbury by-pass) and heading south towards Newbury. Ignore the first junction which leads directly into the town centre. Leave the by-pass at the next junction. Turn right along the A4 towards Hungerford. After passing Halfway House (an eighteenth-century toll house turned pub) turn left down a narrow lane towards Kintbury. The car park is on the

Kintbury church

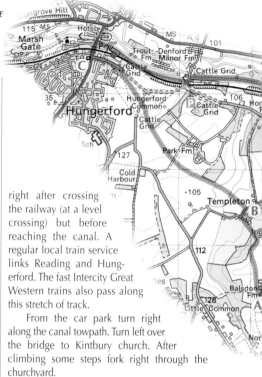

right after crossing
the railway (at a level
crossing) but before
reaching the canal. A
regular local train service
links Reading and Hung-
erford. The fast Intercity Great
Western trains also pass along
this stretch of track.

From the car park turn right
along the canal towpath. Turn left over
the bridge to Kintbury church. After
climbing some steps fork right through the
churchyard.

> St Mary's Church, Kintbury, dates from the thirteenth
> century, although an extensive restoration in 1859 effec-
> tively made it into a Victorian church. The tower has
> recently been restored.

On leaving the churchyard turn right along a track, past
some pretty cottages. Turn left to reach a road, the main
village street.

> Although there are some modern estates built to the
> south of Kintbury above the valley, the old part has
> retained its ancient charm.

Fork left along Wallington Road (towards St Cassian's

Centre). Where the lane bears right continue straight on along a grassy track. At a waymark post, at the barn ahead, turn right across the field. Cross over a track and bear left across the next field. The path is faint but visible (the route passes alongside the wood ahead). After crossing the next stile the path continues straight on between fields, a wide grassy track. Over to the left is St Cassian's College.

St Cassian's College was formerly known as Wallingtons. It was built in the early seventeenth century and features gabled windows on the front and side elevations. The house has been altered to a large extent since it was built.

View across to Walbury Hill

Cross over a drive (leading to St Cassian's) towards the wood ahead. Follow the waymarked path through the wood. On leaving the wood cross the field to a stile in the opposite corner. Turn left along a track. (**A**) At a T-junction turn right along the track, passing to the left of Balsdon Farm. Over to the left is a fine view across the fields towards Walbury Hill. Turn left over a stile just before the track enters the farmyard, to continue along the right-hand side of the field. Cross over a twin stile in the field corner. Bear slightly right across the next field to a public footpath sign on the far side of the field by the wood ahead. Turn right along the field edge. At the field corner turn left over a stile along a track through the pines. Carry straight on past Templeton Stud to reach a lane. Turn right along this lane.

(**B**) At a bend in the road turn sharp left at a public footpath sign, across the field to the hedge gap ahead. In the next field turn right, then left along the right-hand edge of this field. The path then continues between hedges as it gently climbs. At the top of the rise continue straight on over a track. There are more views to the left across to Walbury Hill. Where the field edge bends left continue straight on over a stile across Hungerford Common. Bear right to a public footpath sign by the road ahead. Cross over the road and continue across the common, bearing right to the chapel ahead (now converted to a private house), past a pit on the right. Turn left along the road, past the Down Gate pub, to reach the main street of Hungerford.

The Down Gate pub has a rather amusing notice: 'Can all dogs make sure their owners have clean feet'. Hungerford is a Georgian town, the main High Street being at right angles to the A4. There are still some Georgian shop fronts remaining, while at the northern end of the High Street the houses take on a cottage character. The High Street has a tea room, some shops (if you fancy a picnic by the canal) and several pubs which started out as coaching inns. The walk passes the Three Swans Hotel, which serves bar food. There are a couple of tables by the window facing out onto the High Street.

Opposite the pub is the Town Hall. The town became more and more prosperous in medieval times and became a market town, helped by the busy Bath Road (the A4).

(**C**) Turn right down the High Street. Just before the bridge continue straight on down a gravel path, past some town houses, to reach the Kennet and Avon Canal.

The Kennet and Avon Canal is a combination of three canals that were joined together in the early nineteenth century to provide a continuous waterway from Bristol to London. The final stretch to be completed was from Newbury to Bath, including the 29 locks at Caen Hill. It was a great success and soon became the M4 of its day. The advent of the railways brought a decline in its fortunes, although before nationalisation the Great Western Railway maintained the canal to some extent. From the 1950s the canal fell into disrepair. However it was restored to its former glory thanks to the Kennet and

Along the Kennet and Avon Canal

Dun Mill Lock

Avon Canal Trust, and like others across England has been given a new lease of life at the heart of leisure and tourism.

Turn right along the towpath. Soon the light industry of Hungerford is passed and the path returns to open country, albeit sandwiched between the railway and the A4! At the picturesque Dun Mill Lock the towpath crosses to the north bank of the canal. The path passes along a strip of land between the canal and the River Kennet. At the end of the meadow bear right to a gate to return to the canalside. Further on, the canal passes underneath the railway. Soon the buildings of Kintbury are seen ahead.

In the Middle Ages Kintbury's main industries were centred around the mills of the River Kennet. At one time it held a weekly market and even became larger than Hungerford. The opening of the canal in 1810 brought new industry to Kintbury including iron working, although the town's main source of income was still agriculture, which was controlled by the large manor houses in the nearby countryside.

On the approach to the village pass underneath the bridge leading to the church (crossed on the outward journey) and return to the car park or station.

19: Kintbury and Hamstead Marshall

Distance:	7 miles/11km
Time:	3hr
Map:	OS Landranger 174/Explorer 158
Start:	Car park by Kintbury Station (Grid Ref 385673)
Refreshments:	The Red House, Marsh Benham; The Dundas Arms, Kintbury

START: The canalside car park opposite Kintbury Station. See Walk 18.

From the car park turn right along the canal tow-path. Turn left over the bridge towards Kintbury church. Fork left on entering the churchyard.

Although the church dates from the thirteenth century an extensive restoration in 1859 made it virtually a Victorian church. The tower (also from the thirteenth century) has been recently restored and included a one-light bell opening. Inside the church is a monument to the Craven family who lived at Hamstead Marshall and Ashdown House (see Walk 17) among other places.

The belief in witchcraft prevailed in the Newbury area until the twentieth century. The Kintbury witch together with the church tower were the basis for the legend of the Kintbury Great Bell. During a violent storm part of the tower collapsed and a bell fell into the River Kennet. In order to retrieve it a wizard arranged for a chain to be attached to the bell. This chain was to be pulled by moonlight by twelve white heifers, led by twelve maidens. The job had to be completed in silence or the chain would break. They had almost made it when the Kintbury witch appeared and shouted 'Here comes the Great Kintbury Bell, in spite of all the devils in Hell'. The chain broke and the bell fell back into the river.

Similar in character to Walk 18, this route explores the pastoral farmland between Kintbury and Newbury before returning along the canal. As well as views across to Walbury Hill, the walk includes Hamstead Marshall where the pairs of gateposts standing in the middle of the field are the only remains of the seventeenth-century Hamstead Lodge, which was later destroyed by fire.

On leaving the churchyard continue straight on along the road to reach the village stores. Cross over the High Street and carry on up Inkpen Road, opposite. The road climbs gently, leaving the Kennet Valley and the old part to pass through the not unattractive newer part. Further on, pass Kintbury Newt Pond Nature Reserve. At the top of the rise the road bends right. Turn left by a public footpath sign (by Corbiere and opposite Westridge House). Turn right over a stile and cross the field to a squeeze stile on the top of the ridge (next to a dead tree). Continue straight on across the field.

> Looking back there is a fine view across the Kennet Valley, while over to the right is a view across to Walbury Hill.

Cross over a track and continue alongside a fence on your right, then along the right-hand edge of

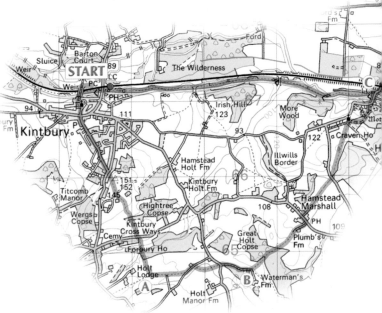

the field, passing a large modern house and its grounds. Bear right over a stile and continue down the left-hand edge of the field (same direction as before). At the bottom cross over a footbridge, then bear left to a stile, the path now returning to the right-hand edge of the field. Cross the next field to reach a lane. Turn left along this lane for a few yards then turn right by a public footpath sign down the right-hand edge of the field. At the bottom bear left over a stile after crossing a stream. Follow the narrow winding path up through the spinney. On emerging from the trees turn right along the right-hand edge of the field.

(**A**) Just before the hedge corner turn left across the field, then along the edge of the field to reach a lane. Opposite a house turn right by a public footpath sign, across a footbridge to a stile. Bear left across two fields via a twin stile in the hedge ahead. In the second field make for a stile in the opposite corner. Turn right along the lane for a few paces, then bear left along a track.

(**B**) Where this track bends right turn left across the field in the direction of a public footpath sign, then along the left-hand edge of the field. In the field corner turn left over a stile, cross over a track, then follow a path through the woods (by a public footpath sign). On leaving the wood continue straight on across the field, bearing right to a stile by a gate below. Continue straight on down the track past Plumb Farm.

The farm is now owned by the National Canine Defence League and includes several kennels. On approaching you will be greeted with a chorus of dogs, who are probably more friendly than they sound!

Turn left along the road in the village of Hamstead Marshall. Opposite is the White Hart Inn. Turn right by a public bridleway sign opposite Elm Farm Research Centre (organic foods and farming). Pass through a gate (which is very stiff to open) and continue between fields to reach a lane. Cross over this lane, bearing left to a stile opposite. Follow a faint path uphill through the scrub.

*Church and gate posts
at Hamstead Marshall*

Looking back, there is another fine view across to Walbury Hill.

At the top, cross over a stile and continue straight on across a long field to Hamstead Marshall church. The path passes to the left of the old gateways.

These old gateways are all that remain of Hamstead Lodge, built for the Earl of Craven by Balthazar Gerbier and completed by Captain Wynne (after Gerbier died in 1663). It was based on Heidelberg Castle to impress the earl's close friend Elizabeth of Bohemia, the 'Winter Queen'. With the earl's help (a staunch Protestant) she became Queen of Bohemia but was deposed by the Habsburgs after just one winter. Elizabeth was the sister of Charles I and the earl was a fervent supporter of the Stuart cause. The house was destroyed by fire in 1718 and these sets of gateposts are all that remain. A new house was built soon afterwards and this is now a nursing home, having been sold by the Craven family in 1984. The church dates from the fourteenth century, although it was later Jacobeanised, Georgianised and

Victorian Gothicised! Inside are some Jacobean and Georgian box pews. The church's main appeal is its location, on top of the ridge with a commanding view across the Kennet Valley.

Turn right along the churchyard wall, then bear right onto a grassy track which winds its way down to the valley. Where the track forks take the left fork. At the bottom bear left to a stile, then turn right along the lane to reach the Kennet and Avon Canal.

Dreweat's Lock

The Kennet and Avon Canal, Kintbury

A short detour along the road brings you to the Red House at Marsh Benham. This was formerly the Water Rat but has now changed hands and been turned into an up-market bar/restaurant with gourmet food. You can relax here in the knowledge that the return to Kintbury is a level stroll along the canal towpath!

(**C**) Turn left along the canal towpath. The towpath runs between the canal and the River Kennet. At Copse Lock the towpath crosses the River Kennet by way of a metal bridge. The canal now passes through a tranquil world of water meadows among pastoral farmland, the peace being shattered only by the trains from the nearby railway. Next is Dreweat's Lock, with a traditional canal bridge.

Here the canal's junction with the Peartree Brook has been made into a 'winding place' where the canalboats can turn around. From the bridge is a fine view across to the North Hampshire Downs. Alongside the canal is a series of pill-boxes placed there in the Second World War. The Kennet and Avon Canal was to become the second line of defence if the south coast were to fall. Thankfully these contingency plans were never put into operation.

After passing Shepherd's Bridge (from which a footpath leads across the fields) Kintbury is soon reached.

Today Kintbury Wharf may seem busy with the numerous pleasure craft passing through it but this is nothing compared to what it was like when the canal first opened. Then it was the centre of the varied industry in Kintbury – iron and coke from South Wales, watercress heading for London, and flour and corn for the mill beside the canal.

Opposite is the Dundas Arms Hotel, named after Charles Dundas, the canal's first chairman. The pub is popular with tourists.

The car park is on the right after crossing the road and passing the lock.

20: Inkpen

Inkpen is the collective name for a group of villages lying in the shadow of Walbury Hill, the highest chalk point in England. At 974ft/297m it is the nearest there is to a mountain in south-east England. There is an Iron Age fort on Walbury Hill and on Combe Gibbet the gallows pole still stands. From the top is a superb view across west Berkshire. Starting from the summit the walk explores some of the villages before a final challenging climb back up to the top.

Distance:	6¼ miles/10.6km
Time:	3hr
Map:	OS Landranger 174/Explorer 158
Start:	Car park on Walbury Hill (Grid Ref 369621)
Refreshments:	The Crown and Garter, Inkpen Common; The Swan Inn, Lower Green

START: The car park on Walbury Hill. The car park is reached from Kintbury (see Walk 18) by following the signs to Inkpen Common and Combe along quiet country lanes.

From the car park turn left along the track across Walbury Hill (heading east).

On Walbury Hill is an Iron Age fort dating from 750 BC. It was built as a tribal centre during the early Iron Age, although later on it may also have been home to a permanent settlement. The hill is privately owned and the track running through the fort is the only means of public access. The track was one of the prehistoric roads/ridgeways and is now known as the Wayfarers' Walk, a recreational path stretching from Inkpen to Emsworth (in Hampshire). From the summit are superb views across west Berkshire to the north and Hampshire to the south.

Ignore two public footpaths going off left and right. When a road is reached cross over it and pass through the metal gate opposite. Follow a faint track across the field, firstly making for the corner of the wood ahead, then bearing right to cross the field to a bridlegate on the far side (keeping above the scrub).

Over to the left the ramparts of Walbury Fort are seen.

After passing through the bridlegate carry on down the lane. (**A**) Turn left along a track by a public bridleway sign. Further on, ignore a public footpath going off to the left. Turn left along the farm drive. Turn left along a lane. At a T-junction turn right. (To visit West Woodhay church turn left here.) (**B**) At a public footpath sign turn sharp left across the field in the direction of West Woodhay church. Make for a stile by the churchyard.

West Woodhay church was built in 1883, the third church in the village. The church was moved away from West Woodhay House when it was rebuilt for the second time. The east window includes a design by Sir Edward Burne-Jones depicting the Crucifixion. The church contains a number of memorials to the Cole family who owned the estate until the 1920s, when it passed to the Hendersons. The memorial garden next to the churchyard is in memory of Mrs Sarah Henderson who was killed in a hunting accident in 1972.

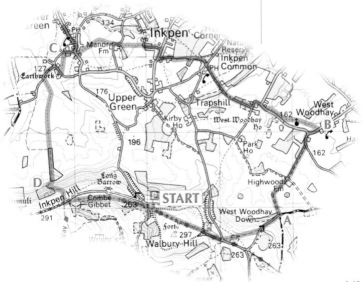

Walbury Hill

Continue along the left-hand edge of the field. At the hedge corner carry straight on across the field to reach a lane. Turn right along this lane, past West Woodhay House.

> West Woodhay House was built in 1635, although according to Pevsner it looks much later (c1675) when viewed from afar (such as across the lake from this lane).

Follow the lane round to the left. Turn right along a track between two avenues of pines. Further on, the track becomes gravelled before arriving at the Crown and Garter pub on Inkpen Common. Cross over the lane by the pub and continue straight on along the track opposite. Where the track forks take the left fork along the inside edge of the wood. Further on, the track emerges alongside some cottages. By the second cottage turn right through a kissing gate (by a public footpath sign) across the meadow to reach a road. Continue straight on along the lane opposite.

At the end of the lane pass through a gate, the track soon bending right. Turn left by a public footpath sign, first alongside the fence on the left, then straight across the field to a stile to the right of the farm buildings ahead. Continue straight on along the lane, then straight on over a stile when the lane bends left (between the farm buildings). Turn left to a gate next to the farm buildings, then turn right along a permissive path between a fence and hedge (the official right of way cuts across the field). Further on, the path bends left to a kissing gate. Follow a narrow path through the scrub (this becomes overgrown in summer). Later the path swings to the left to come out to a drive leading to a lane in Lower Green.

> Lower Green is one of the villages making up the group of settlements collectively known as Inkpen. Turning right, then left, past the village green brings you to the Swan Inn, an excellent pub which serves only organic food. Alongside the pub is an organic farm shop.

To continue the walk, turn left, then right along the road signposted to Ham and Shalbourne. (**C**) Turn left by a public footpath sign to a stile. Pass alongside the fence

Walbury Hill Fort

West Woodhay church

on your left to reach a further stile, then bear left across the second field to a stile by a metal gate. For Inkpen church turn left, then right.

Inkpen church dates from the mid-thirteenth century and was rebuilt in 1896–97, adding a new aisle, altar and the elaborate rood screen. This was carved from two mature oak trees from the nearby Kirby Estate. The screen contains a large foliaged cross with the symbols of the four evangelists on its arms. A near life-size carving of the crucified Christ is nailed to the cross. When the church was restored there were traces of some medieval wall paintings found underneath the plaster. These were too far gone to be restored so some new paintings were completed in 1910 by Miss Ethel King Martin. The new paintings are of the Annunciation (south chancel wall),

First Christmas (north chancel wall), angels of healing and light (nave arches) and the Ascension (on the south wall near the door). A new brochure for the third millennium proudly states that the church is a 'place of prayer and worship for all, open seven days a week, lovingly maintained and beautifully decorated'.

On leaving the church turn left down the lane, then left at the T-junction at the bottom. Turn left along the track (by a public footpath sign) just after leaving the village. This track climbs towards the chalk scarp ahead. Further on, ignore a track going off to the right.

Alongside this track traces of the foundations of a dwelling of the Knights Hospitallers have been found when ploughing. The area is known as Bunjam (from the French *bons hommes* – good men). The Wansdyke, an earthwork that once stretched across the North Wiltshire Downs to the River Severn, began here. It is still visible on parts of the Marlborough Downs.

Inkpen church

147

Further on, the path bends left to a bridlegate. Here turn right, straight up the scarp, to reach a faint track – there are footholds to assist you in places. Turn left along this track, climbing towards the top. Further on, the track swings right. At the top bear right to a bridlegate, then on to a further metal gate. (**D**) Turn left along the track towards Combe Gibbet.

> The gibbet was erected on top of a Neolithic long barrow in 1676 for the hanging of George Broomham (of Inkpen) and Dorothy Newman (of Combe) for the murder of Broomham's wife and son (Dorothy Newman was his mistress). The gibbet was never used again, although it has been maintained and has now become a local landmark.
>
> The Neolithic long barrow dates from about 3500 BC. It was built as a burial mound. Inside there were several chambers where the ashes of the dead person were placed with some of his or her most treasured possessions.

From the gibbet continue along the track back to the car park.

Postscript

A mile or so to the west of Combe Gibbet you arrive in Wiltshire, the county of legend, chalk horses, prehistoric monuments and a whole lot besides. Wiltshire is renowned for its eight chalk horses but on the Downs near Ham (about half a mile to the west of this walk) there once was a ninth. It was shown on the 1870s Ordnance Survey 6 inch map (1:10,560). Apparently the horse was made only by cutting the grass back to the chalk. Although the owners of the time maintained the horse, by 1922 the next owners let the grass grow back and the horse disappeared.

Appendix A: Useful Addresses

Tourist information centres:

The Look Out Discovery Centre
Nine Mile Ride
BRACKNELL
RG12 7QW
Tel: 01344 354400
Fax: 01344 354422
Email: TheLookOut@bracknell-forest.gov.uk
www.bracknell-forest.gov.uk

Easthampstead House
Town Square
BRACKNELL
RG12 1AQ

Maidenhead Information Centre
Central Library
St Ives Road
MAIDENHEAD
SL6 1QU
Tel: 01628 781110
Email: maidenhead.tic@rbwm.gov.uk
www.maidenhead.gov.uk

The Wharf
NEWBURY
RG14 5AS
Tel: 01635 30267
Fax: 01635 519562
Email: tourism@westberks.gov.uk

Royal Windsor Information Centre
24 High Street
WINDSOR
SL4 1LH
Tel: 01753 743900
Fax: 01753 743904
Email: windsor.tic@rbwm.gov.uk
www.windsor.gov.uk

West Berkshire Council leisure and tourism:

www.westberkshire/ tourism.nsf

Appendix B: Further Reading

John Betjeman and John Piper (eds), *Murray's Berkshire Architectural Guide* (John Murray, 1949)

Nikolaus Pevsner, *The Buildings of England: Berkshire* (Penguin, 1966)

AA Book of British Villages (Drive Publications, 1980)

Folklore Myths and Legends of Britain (Readers Digest, 1973)

G A J Goodhart, *Inkpen – Church and Village* (1994)

The Church of St Michael and All Angels, Inkpen. The Third Millennium (2000)

Aldworth Church – Visitors' Guide (1966)

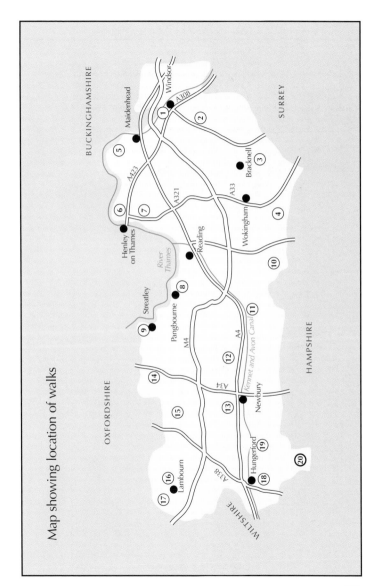

Map showing location of walks

NOTES

LISTING OF CICERONE GUIDES

NORTHERN ENGLAND LONG DISTANCE TRAILS
- THE DALES WAY
- THE ISLE OF MAN COASTAL PATH
- THE PENNINE WAY
- THE ALTERNATIVE COAST TO COAST
- NORTHERN COAST-TO-COAST
- THE RELATIVE HILLS OF BRITAIN
- MOUNTAINS ENGLAND & WALES
  VOL 1 WALES
  VOL 2 ENGLAND

CYCLING
- BORDER COUNTRY BIKE ROUTES
- THE CHESHIRE CYCLE WAY
- THE CUMBRIA CYCLE WAY
- THE DANUBE CYCLE WAY
- LANDS END TO JOHN O'GROATS CYCLE GUIDE
- ON THE RUFFSTUFF – 84 BIKE RIDES IN NORTH ENGLAND
- RURAL RIDES NO.1 WEST SURREY
- RURAL RIDES NO.1 EAST SURREY
- SOUTH LAKELAND CYCLE RIDES
- THE WAY OF ST JAMES LE PUY TO SANTIAGO – CYCLIST'S
- CYCLE TOURING IN SPAIN
- THE LOIRE CYCLE ROUTE

LAKE DISTRICT AND MORECAMBE BAY
- CONISTON COPPER MINES
- CUMBRIA WAY & ALLERDALE RAMBLE
- THE CHRONICLES OF MILNTHORPE
- THE EDEN WAY
- FROM FELL AND FIELD
- KENDAL – A SOCIAL HISTORY
- A LAKE DISTRICT ANGLER'S GUIDE
- LAKELAND TOWNS
- LAKELAND VILLAGES
- LAKELAND PANORAMAS
- THE LOST RESORT?
- SCRAMBLES IN THE LAKE DISTRICT
- MORE SCRAMBLES IN THE LAKE DISTRICT
- SHORT WALKS IN LAKELAND
  BOOK 1: SOUTH
  BOOK 2: NORTH
  BOOK 3: WEST
- ROCKY RAMBLER'S WILD WALKS
- RAIN OR SHINE
- ROADS AND TRACKS OF THE LAKE DISTRICT
- THE TARNS OF LAKELAND VOL 1: WEST
- THE TARNS OF LAKELAND VOL 2: EAST
- WALKING ROUND THE LAKES
- WALKS SILVERDALE/ARNSIDE
- WINTER CLIMBS IN LAKE DISTRICT

NORTH-WEST ENGLAND
- WALKING IN CHESHIRE
- FAMILY WALKS IN FOREST OF BOWLAND
- WALKING IN THE FOREST OF BOWLAND
- LANCASTER CANAL WALKS

- WALKER'S GUIDE TO LANCASTER CANAL
- CANAL WALKS VOL 1: NORTH
- WALKS FROM THE LEEDS-LIVERPOOL CANAL
- THE RIBBLE WAY
- WALKS IN RIBBLE COUNTRY
- WALKING IN LANCASHIRE
- WALKS ON THE WEST PENNINE MOORS
- WALKS IN LANCASHIRE WITCH COUNTRY
- HADRIAN'S WALL
  VOL 1 : THE WALL WALK
  VOL 2 : WALL COUNTRY WALKS

NORTH-EAST ENGLAND
- NORTH YORKS MOORS
- THE REIVER'S WAY
- THE TEESDALE WAY
- WALKING IN COUNTY DURHAM
- WALKING IN THE NORTH PENNINES
- WALKING IN NORTHUMBERLAND
- WALKING IN THE WOLDS
- WALKS IN THE NORTH YORK MOORS BOOKS 1 AND 2
- WALKS IN THE YORKSHIRE DALES BOOKS 1,2 AND 3
- WALKS IN DALES COUNTRY
- WATERFALL WALKS – TEESDALE & HIGH PENNINES
- THE YORKSHIRE DALES
- YORKSHIRE DALES ANGLER'S GUIDE

THE PEAK DISTRICT
- STAR FAMILY WALKS PEAK DISTRICT/STH YORKS
- HIGH PEAK WALKS
- WEEKEND WALKS IN THE PEAK DISTRICT
- WHITE PEAK WALKS
  VOL.1 NORTHERN DALES
  VOL.2 SOUTHERN DALES
- WHITE PEAK WAY
- WALKING IN PEAKLAND
- WALKING IN SHERWOOD FOREST
- WALKING IN STAFFORDSHIRE
- THE VIKING WAY

WALES AND WELSH BORDERS
- ANGLESEY COAST WALKS
- ASCENT OF SNOWDON
- THE BRECON BEACONS
- CLWYD ROCK
- HEREFORD & THE WYE VALLEY
- HILLWALKING IN SNOWDONIA
- HILLWALKING IN WALES VOL.1
- HILLWALKING IN WALES VOL.2
- LLEYN PENINSULA COASTAL PATH
- WALKING OFFA'S DYKE PATH
- THE PEMBROKESHIRE COASTAL PATH
- THE RIDGES OF SNOWDONIA
- SARN HELEN
- SCRAMBLES IN SNOWDONIA
- SEVERN WALKS
- THE SHROPSHIRE HILLS
- THE SHROPSHIRE WAY
- SPIRIT PATHS OF WALES
- WALKING DOWN THE WYE

- A WELSH COAST TO COAST WALK
  •WELSH WINTER CLIMBS

THE MIDLANDS
- CANAL WALKS VOL 2: MIDLANDS
- THE COTSWOLD WAY
- COTSWOLD WALKS
  BOOK 1: NORTH
  BOOK 2: CENTRAL
  BOOK 3: SOUTH
- THE GRAND UNION CANAL WALK
- HEART OF ENGLAND WALKS
- WALKING IN OXFORDSHIRE
- WALKING IN WARWICKSHIRE
- WALKING IN WORCESTERSHIRE
- WEST MIDLANDS ROCK

SOUTH AND SOUTH-WEST ENGLAND
- WALKING IN BEDFORDSHIRE
- WALKING IN BUCKINGHAMSHIRE
- CHANNEL ISLAND WALKS
- CORNISH ROCK
- WALKING IN CORNWALL
- WALKING IN THE CHILTERNS
- WALKING ON DARTMOOR
- WALKING IN DEVON
- WALKING IN DORSET
- CANAL WALKS VOL 3: SOUTH
- EXMOOR & THE QUANTOCKS
- THE GREATER RIDGEWAY
- WALKING IN HAMPSHIRE
- THE ISLE OF WIGHT
- THE KENNET & AVON WALK
- THE LEA VALLEY WALK
- LONDON: THE DEFINITIVE WALKING GUIDE
- LONDON THEME WALKS
- THE NORTH DOWNS WAY
- THE SOUTH DOWNS WAY
- THE ISLES OF SCILLY
- THE SOUTHERN COAST TO COAST
- SOUTH WEST COAST PATH
- WALKING IN SOMERSET
- WALKING IN SUSSEX
- THE THAMES PATH
- TWO MOORS WAY
- WALKS IN KENT BOOK 1
- WALKS IN KENT BOOK 2
- THE WEALDWAY & VANGUARD WAY

SCOTLAND
- WALKING IN THE ISLE OF ARRAN
- THE BORDER COUNTRY – A WALKERS GUIDE
- BORDER COUNTRY CYCLE ROUTES
- BORDER PUBS & INNS – A WALKERS' GUIDE
- CAIRNGORMS, WINTER CLIMBS 5TH EDITION
- CENTRAL HIGHLANDS 6 LONG DISTANCE WALKS
- WALKING THE GALLOWAY HILLS
- WALKING IN THE HEBRIDES
- NORTH TO THE CAPE
- THE ISLAND OF RHUM